AIKI-JO
AN ILLUSTRATED HANDBOOK

Other Aikido books by Nick Waites

All available from Amazon.com

Aikido and Kuzushi
Koteikan Press, 2016

Kokyu Nage – An Illustrated Handbook
Koteikan Press, 2017

Progressive Aikido – An Illustrated Handbook
Koteikan Press, 2017

Aikido Concepts and principles
Koteikan Press, 2017

AIKI-JO

An Illustrated Handbook

by Nick Waites

Kōteikan Press 2017

Copyright © 2017 by Nick Waites

All rights reserved. This book or any portion thereof may not be reproduced or used in any manner whatsoever without the express written permission of the publisher except for the use of brief quotations in a book review or scholarly journal.

First Printing: 2014

ISBN: 9781549881251

Koteikan Press

www.aikido-koteikan.co.uk

Contents

Acknowledgements vii
Japanese Aikido terms vii
Introduction 1

Part 1: Preparatory exercises 3
Jo swinging exercise 1: Single arm swing 4
Jo swinging exercise 2: Alternating arm swing 5
Jo stretching exercise 1: Side stretch 6
Jo stretching exercise 2: Shoulder stretch #1 7
Jo stretching exercise 3: Shoulder stretch #2 8

Part 2: Suburi 9
Choku tsuki 10
Kaeshi tsuki 11
Jodan tsuki 12
Ushiro tsuki #1 13
Ushiro tsuki #2 14
Tenkan ushiro tsuki 15
Men gaeshi renzoku 16
Shomen uchikomi 16
Shomen uchikomi #2 18
Gyaku yokomen uchi 19
Yoko gedan gaeshi 20
Choku tsuki gedan gaeshi 20
Toma katate uchi 22
Toma katate gedan gaeshi 23
Hasso gaeshi 24
Irimi tenkan hasso gaeshi 25
Hasso gaeshi shomen uchi 25
Hasso ushiro gaeshi 27
Hasso gaeshi ushiro uchi 28
Hasso ushiro tsuki 29
Hachi no ji 30
Hachi no ji ushiro tsuki 30

Part 3: Kata 33
Nana no kata (7 count kata) 34
Ju san no kata (13 count kata) 37
San ju ichi no kata (31 count kata) 41

Part 4: Jo dori 49
Kokyu nage #1 50
Kokyu nage #2 51
Kokyu nage #3 52
Kokyu nage #4 53
Kokyu nage #5 54
Kokyu nage #6 55
Kote gaeshi 56
Shiho nage 57
Ikkyo 58

Part 5: Jo waza 59
Kokyu ho #1 60
Kokyu ho #2 61
Kokyu nage #1 62

Kokyu nage #2	63
Kokyu nage #3	64
Kokyu nage #4	65
Kokyu nage #5	66
Kokyu nage #6	67
Kokyu nage #7	68
Kata gatame	69
Nikyo	70
Sankyo	72
Shiho nage	73
Part 6: Kumijo	**75**
Kumijo #1	76
Kumijo #2	77
Kumijo #3	78
Kumijo #4	79
Kumijo #5	80
Kumijo #6	81
Kumijo #7	82
Kumijo #8	83
Kumijo #9	84
Kumijo #10	85
Kumijo #11	86
Paired sequence Part 1	87
Paired sequence Part 2	91
Glossary	**100**

Acknowledgements

My special thanks go to Shaun Carr and Margaret Turner who patiently assisted me with photographic sessions, and to Jason Smith for his photographic skills.

Japanese Aikido terms

The Japanese terms used throughout this book are shown in italics and are listed in the Glossary, along with an approximate pronunciation guide.

Introduction

The *jo*, an approximately four foot long wooden stave, is a rather innocuous weapon, its versatility and effectiveness not immediately apparent. However, in the right hands it can be used to devastating effect as Miyamoto Musashi the very famous Japanese swordsman discovered in a match with Musō Gonnosuke Katsuyoshi, another famous martial artist. If the account is to be believed, Katsuyoshi beat Musashi using only a *jo*, the only time Musashi was defeated; true or not, the *jo* is still regarded as a formidable weapon.

The use of the *jo* features in most *Aikido dojos*. It is important in its own right as a weapon of offence and defence, but perhaps just as importantly as a supplement to *Aikido* unarmed training. *Aiki-jo* training reinforces *tai sabaki*, reaction speed, distance awareness and many other basic principles of *Aikido* practice. Moreover, *jo suburi* and *jo kata* forms of practice are performed solo, without the need for a training partner.

In this volume we provide illustrated guidance to six forms of *Aiki-jo* training:

- Part 1 deals with preliminary exercises to loosen the body and become familiar with handling the *jo*.
- In Part 2 we describe over 20 forms of *jo suburi*, that is basic exercises for attack and defence.
- Part 3 builds on Part 2 by presenting three commonly practised *jo kata* that incorporate *suburi* in continuous sequences.
- Partner practice in Part 4 shows techniques where *uke*, wielding the *jo*, attacks *tori* who disarms and throws or pins *uke*. This form of practice is termed *jo dori*.
- In Part 5, *jo waza*, *tori* throws or immobilises *uke* using the *jo*.
- Finally in Part 6 *tori* and *uke*, both wielding a *jo*, are shown performing paired exercises, that is *kumijo*, before demonstrating a continuous sequence of mutual attacks and defences.

Aiki-jo forms are all beneficial to basic unarmed *Aikido* training, but they are much more than that; they also enrich the *Aikido* training experience, making it as exciting as it is enjoyable.

Part 1: Preparatory exercises

In this part of the book three stretching and two swinging exercises are illustrated. To help to clarify the swinging exercises, one end of the *jo* has been marked so that rotations of the *jo* are more clearly shown, and arrows are included to show the intended trajectory of the *jo*.

Jo swinging exercise 1: Single arm swing

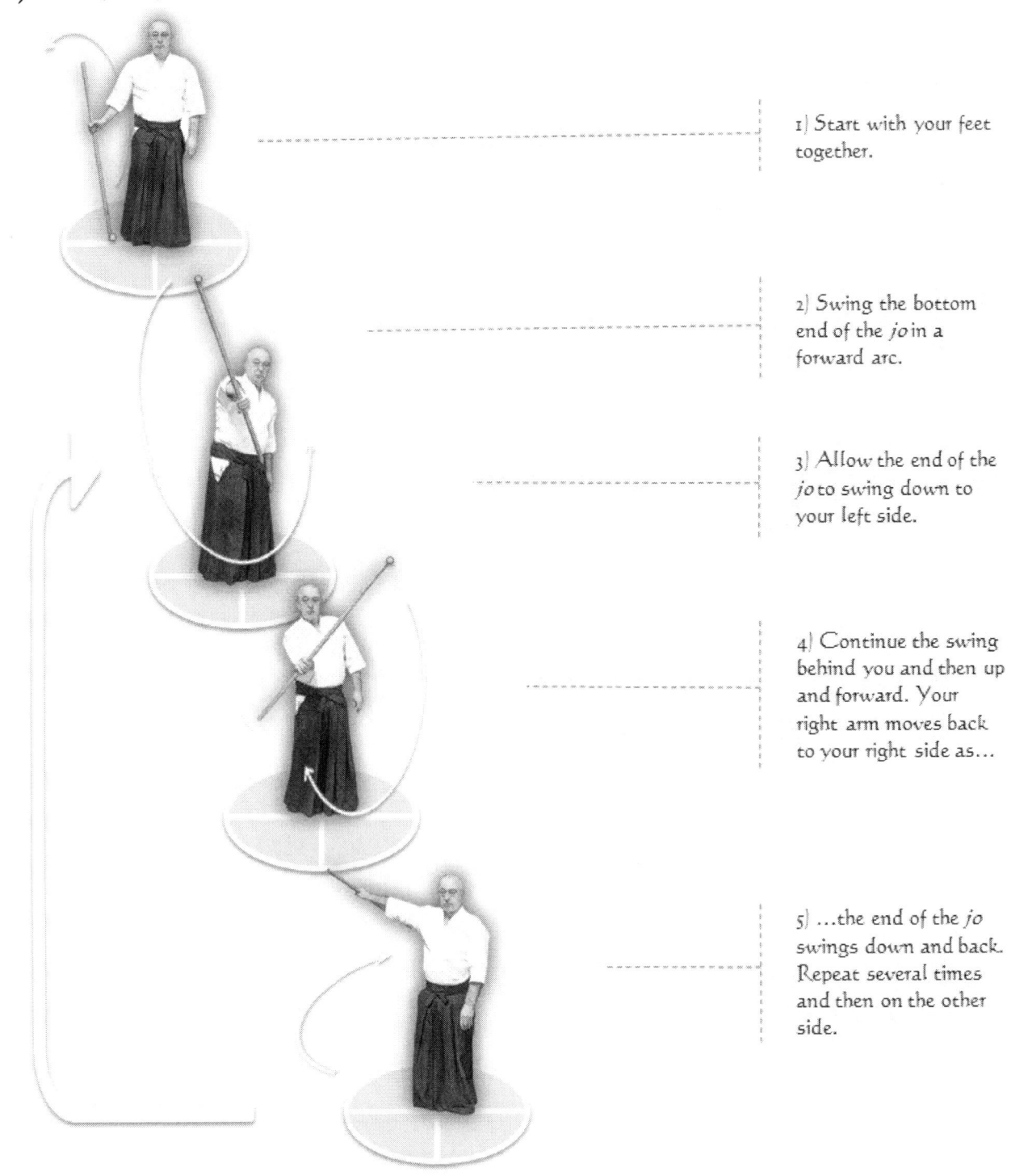

1) Start with your feet together.

2) Swing the bottom end of the *jo* in a forward arc.

3) Allow the end of the *jo* to swing down to your left side.

4) Continue the swing behind you and then up and forward. Your right arm moves back to your right side as…

5) …the end of the *jo* swings down and back. Repeat several times and then on the other side.

JO SWINGING EXERCISE 2: ALTERNATING ARM SWING

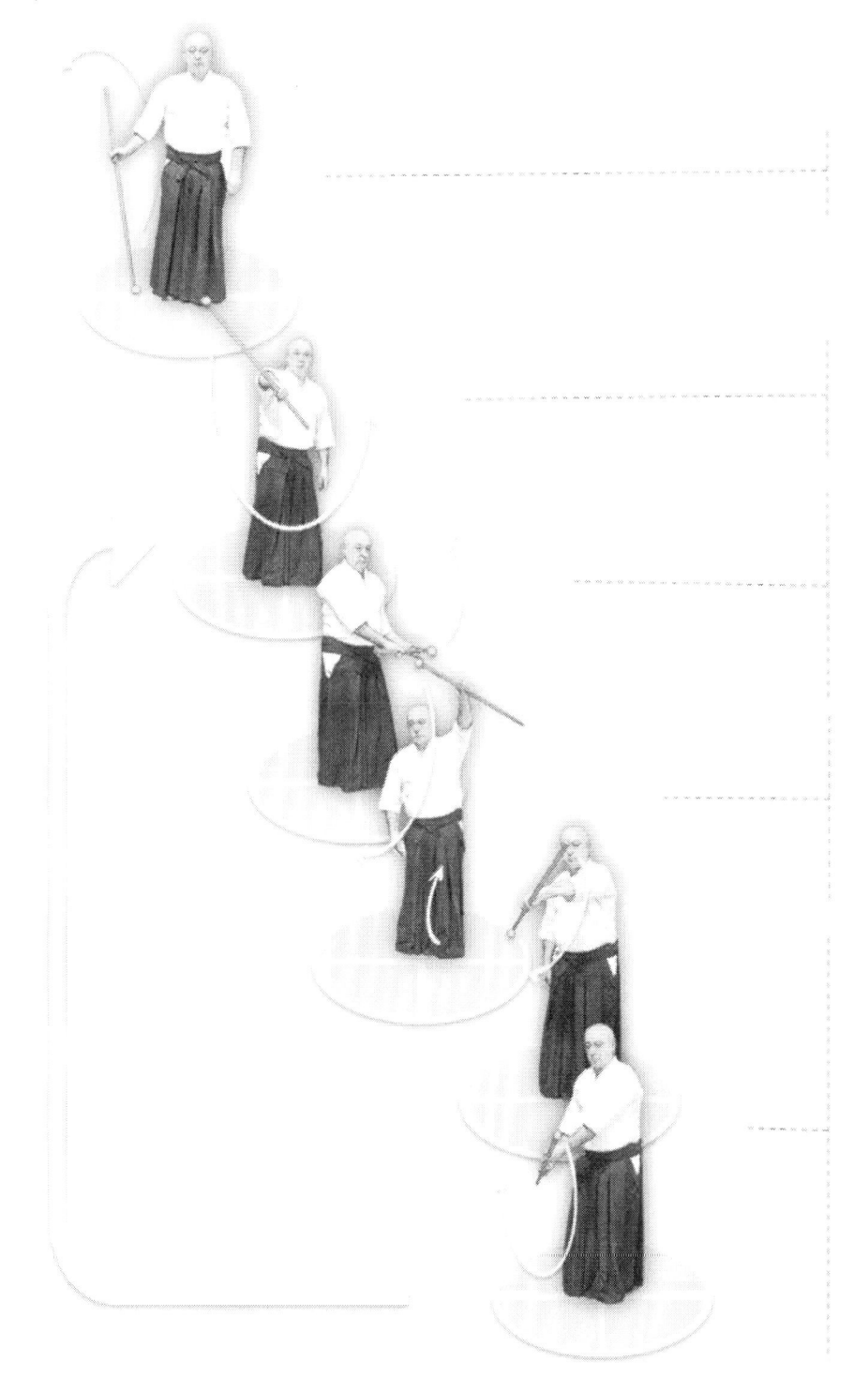

1) Start with your feet together.

2) Swing the bottom end of the *jo* in a forward arc.

3) Allow the end of the *jo* to swing down to your left side, take hold of it with your left hand from underneath and release your right hand grip.

4) As the *jo* spins in your left hand swing your left arm forward and in front of you so that the bottom end swings in a forward arc.

5) Allow the *jo* to spin 360° at your right side, take hold from underneath and release your left hand grip. Repeat.

Part 1: Preparatory exercises

JO STRETCHING EXERCISE 1: SIDE STRETCH

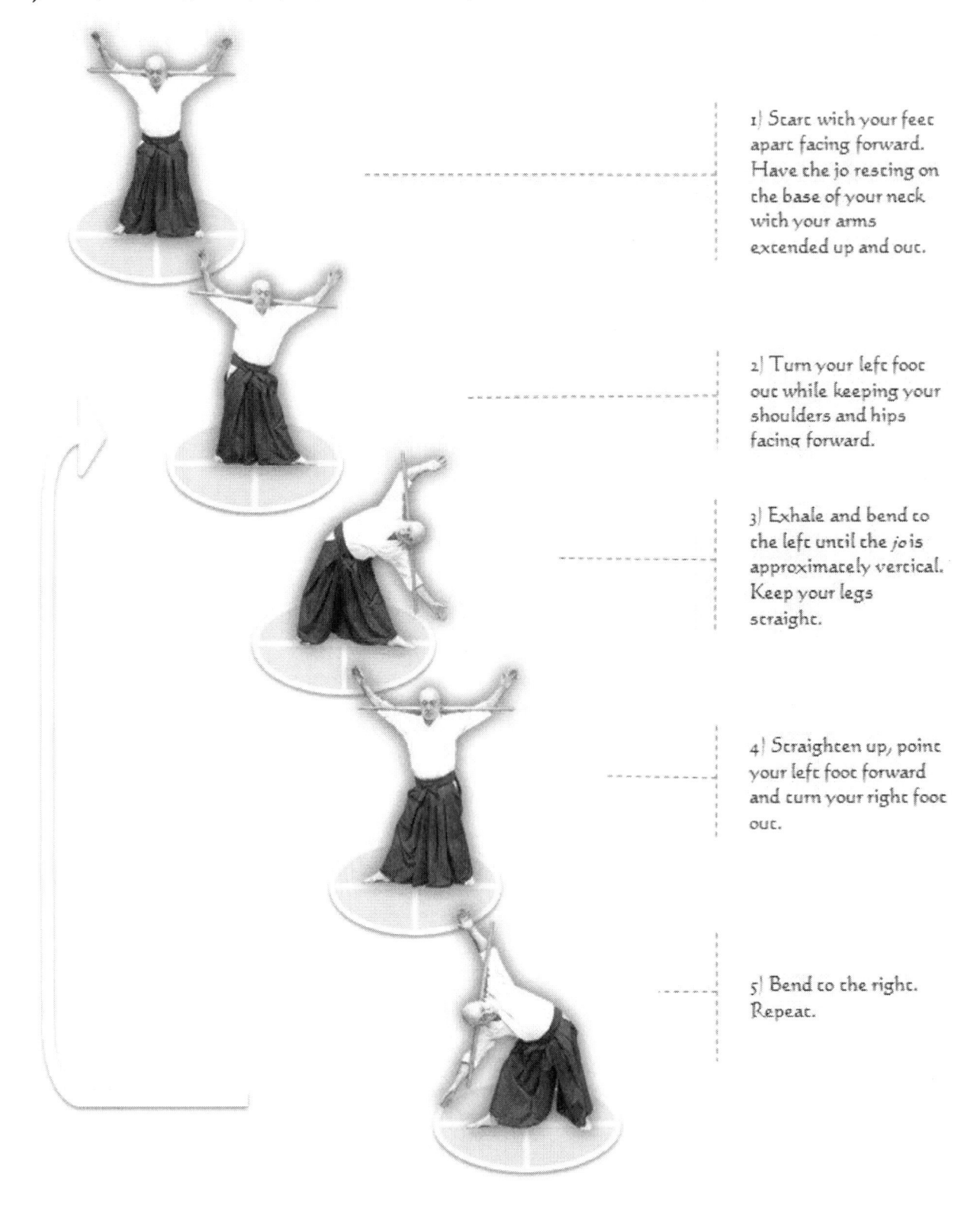

1) Start with your feet apart facing forward. Have the jo resting on the base of your neck with your arms extended up and out.

2) Turn your left foot out while keeping your shoulders and hips facing forward.

3) Exhale and bend to the left until the *jo* is approximately vertical. Keep your legs straight.

4) Straighten up, point your left foot forward and turn your right foot out.

5) Bend to the right. Repeat.

[6]

Part 1: Preparatory exercises

Jo stretching exercise 2: Shoulder stretch #1

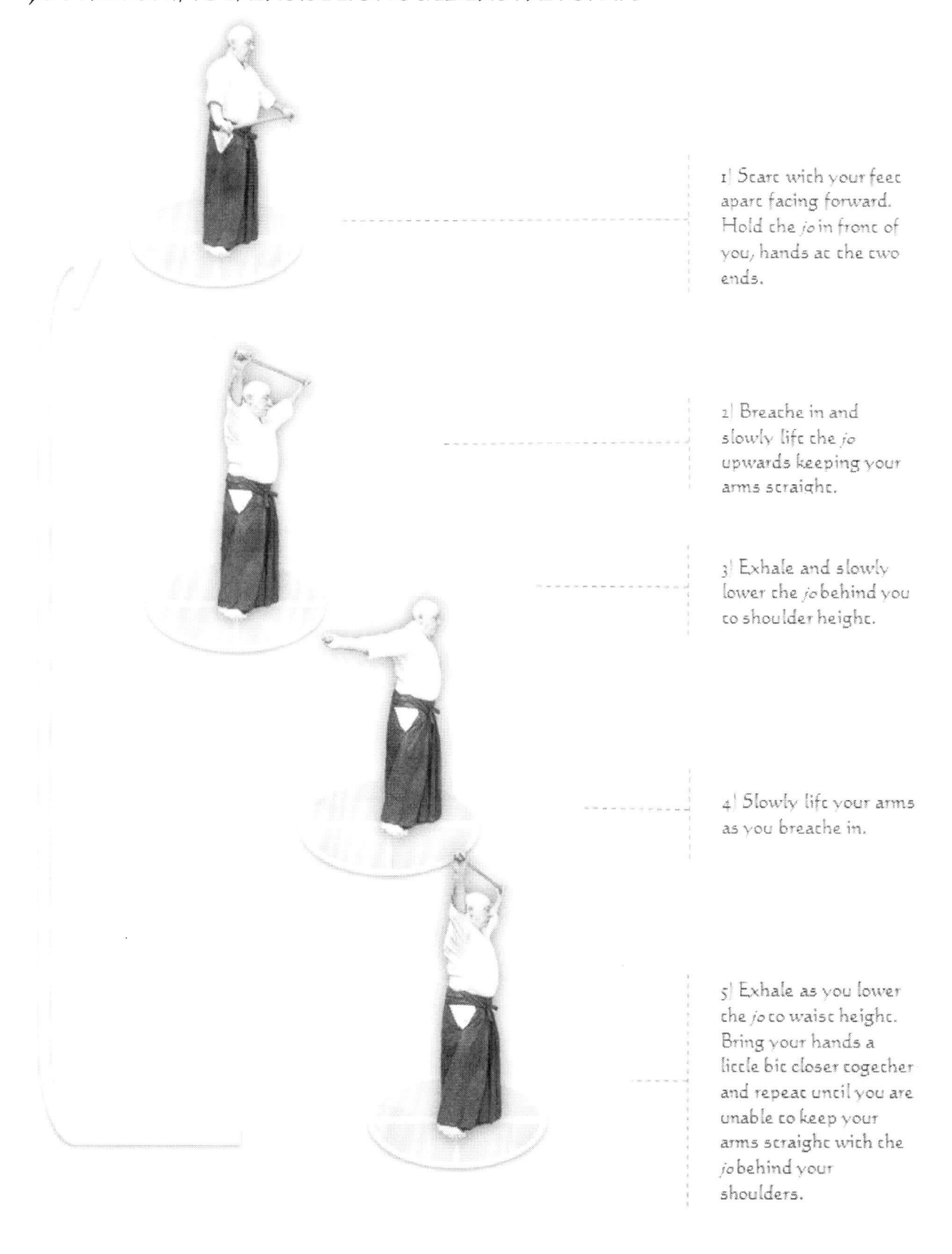

1) Start with your feet apart facing forward. Hold the *jo* in front of you, hands at the two ends.

2) Breathe in and slowly lift the *jo* upwards keeping your arms straight.

3) Exhale and slowly lower the *jo* behind you to shoulder height.

4) Slowly lift your arms as you breathe in.

5) Exhale as you lower the *jo* to waist height. Bring your hands a little bit closer together and repeat until you are unable to keep your arms straight with the *jo* behind your shoulders.

Jo stretching exercise 3: Shoulder stretch #2

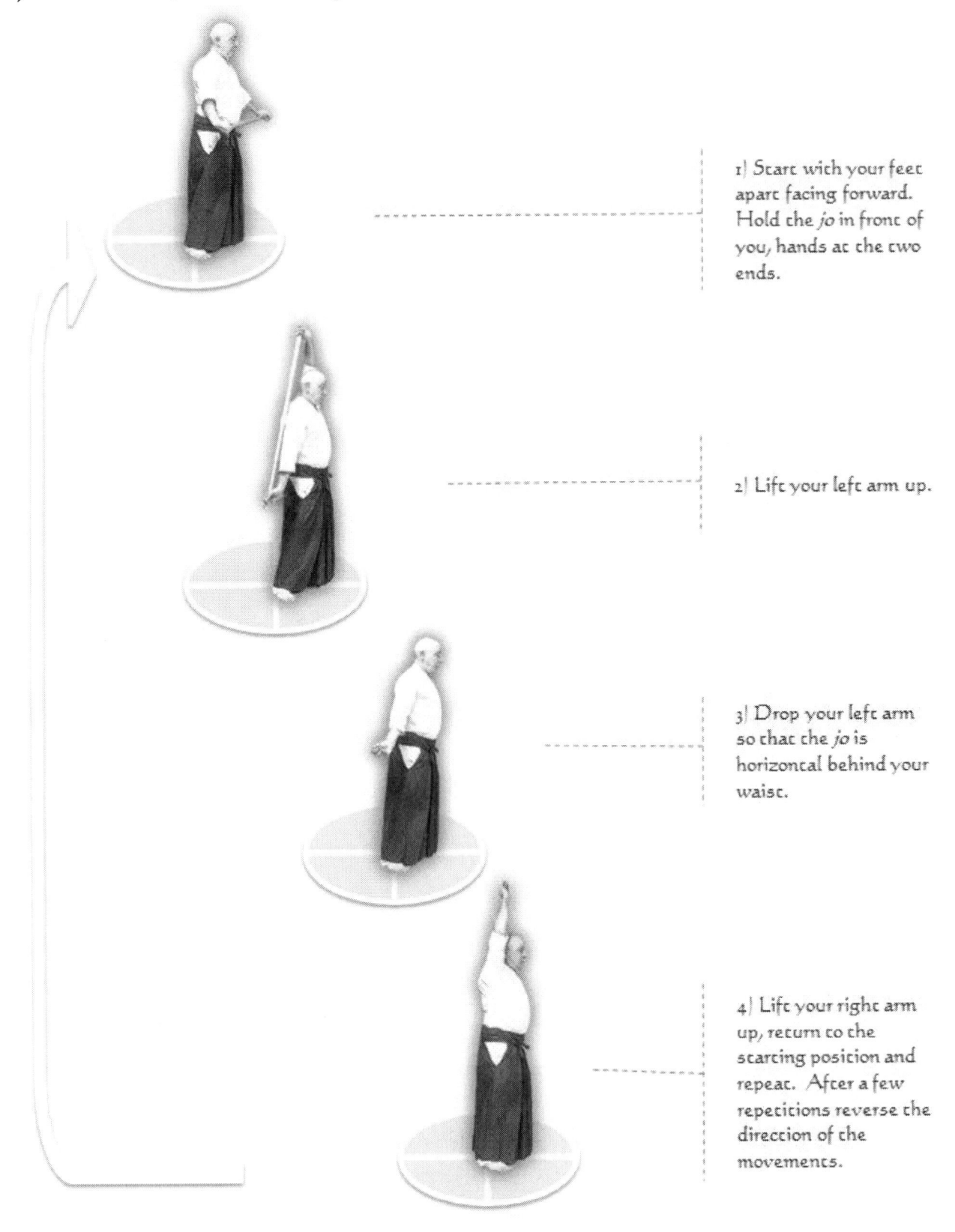

1) Start with your feet apart facing forward. Hold the *jo* in front of you, hands at the two ends.

2) Lift your left arm up.

3) Drop your left arm so that the *jo* is horizontal behind your waist.

4) Lift your right arm up, return to the starting position and repeat. After a few repetitions reverse the direction of the movements.

Part 2: Suburi

The *suburi* illustrated in this section include many of the attack and defence forms practised in *Aikido dojos*. Before progressing to the three *kata* in the next section it is advisable to practice these *suburi* until they are very familiar; then learning the *kata* will be much easier.

Choku tsuki

1) Stand in *hidari hanmi*

2) Swing the lower end of the *jo* into your right hand.

3) Lift your right arm to about head height.

4) As you step forward (*okuri ashi*) swing the *jo* to the horizontal and slide it forwards and through your left hand. Your hands rotate so that the heel of your left hand faces downwards. You finish with your front knee bent and back leg straight.

Kaeshi tsuki

1) Stand in *hidari hanmi*

2) Take hold of the top end of the *jo* with your right hand.

3) Slide forward (*okuri ashi*) and thrust at *jodan* level.

Jodan tsuki

1) Stand in *hidari hanmi*.

2) Lift the *jo* to an approximately vertical position, with your left hand holding the lower end at your centre.

3) Slide forward (*okuri ashi*) and thrust at *jodan* level.

Part 2: Suburi

USHIRO TSUKI #1

1) Stand in *hidari hanmi*.

2) Swing the lower end of the *jo* into your right hand.

3) Slide your left hand to the end of the *jo*.

4) Move to your rear (*ushiro tsuki ashi*) as you slide the *jo* through your right to thrust backwards.

[13]

Ushiro tsuki #2

1) Stand in *hidari hanmi*

2) Lift the *jo* to a vertical position with your right hand, sliding it through your left hand.

3) Step back.

4) Move further to your rear as you thrust the *jo* backwards.

Tenkan ushiro tsuki

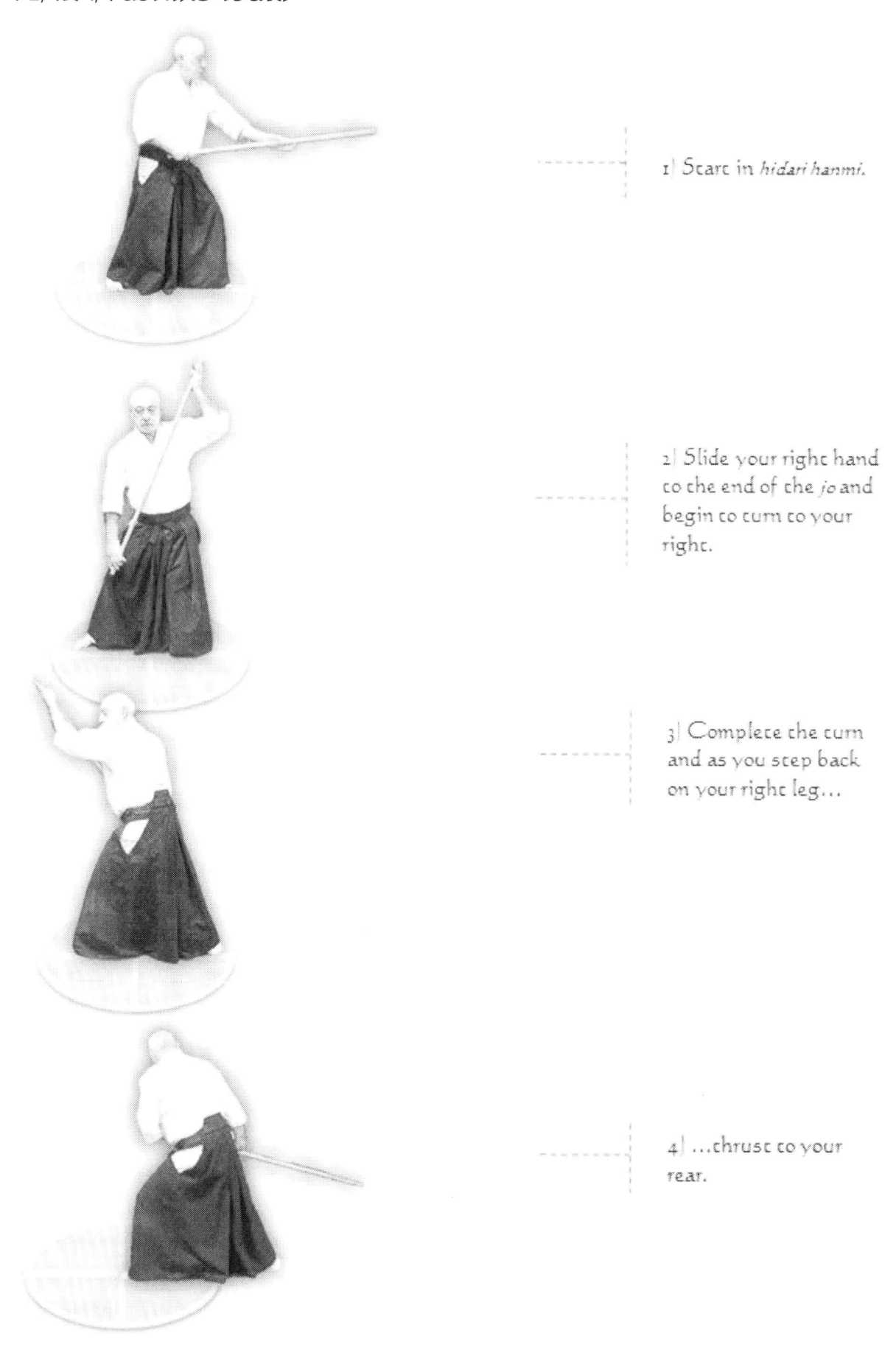

1) Start in *hidari hanmi*.

2) Slide your right hand to the end of the *jo* and begin to turn to your right.

3) Complete the turn and as you step back on your right leg...

4) ...thrust to your rear.

Men gaeshi renzoku

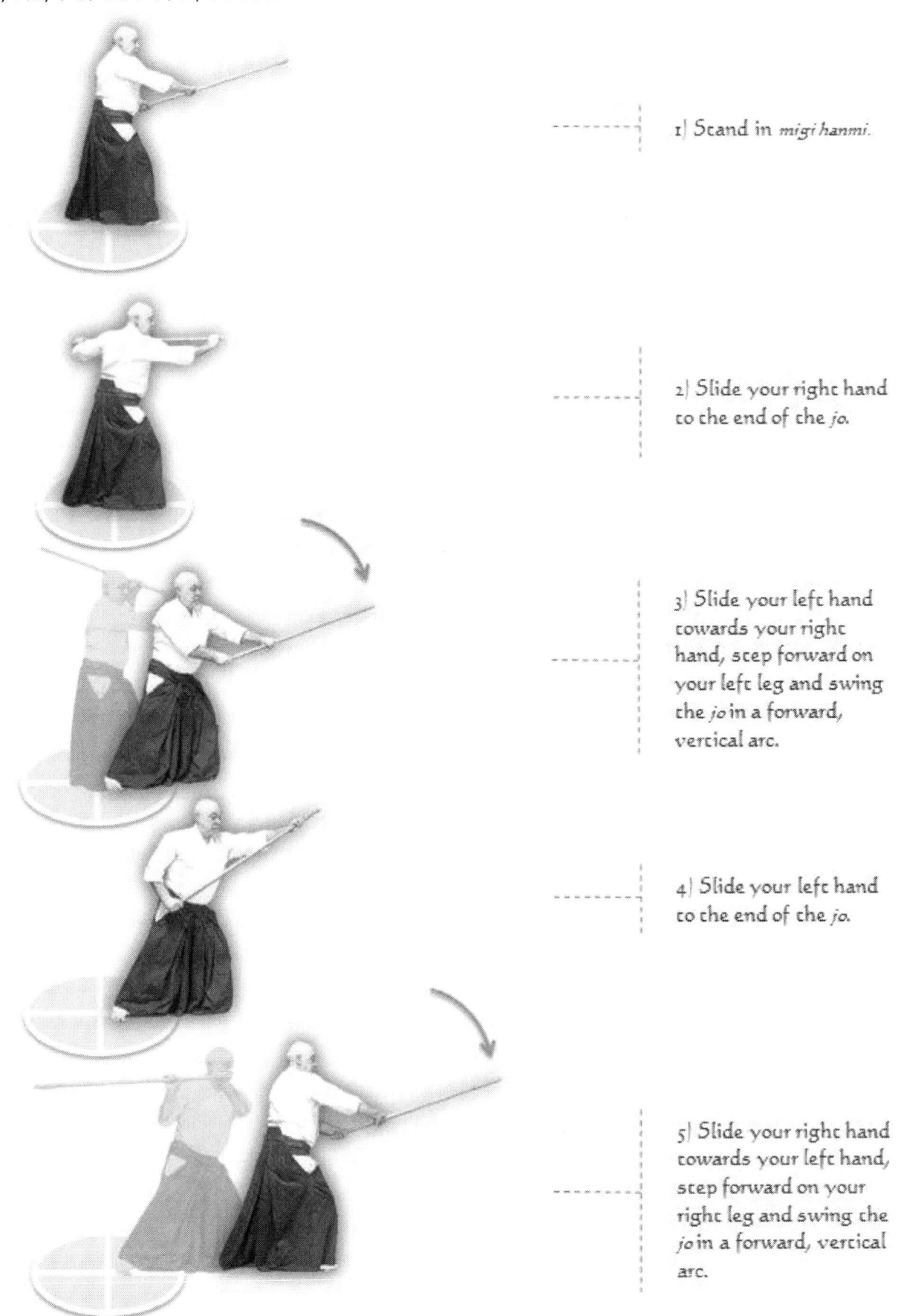

1) Stand in *migi hanmi*.

2) Slide your right hand to the end of the *jo*.

3) Slide your left hand towards your right hand, step forward on your left leg and swing the *jo* in a forward, vertical arc.

4) Slide your left hand to the end of the *jo*.

5) Slide your right hand towards your left hand, step forward on your right leg and swing the *jo* in a forward, vertical arc.

Shomen uchikomi

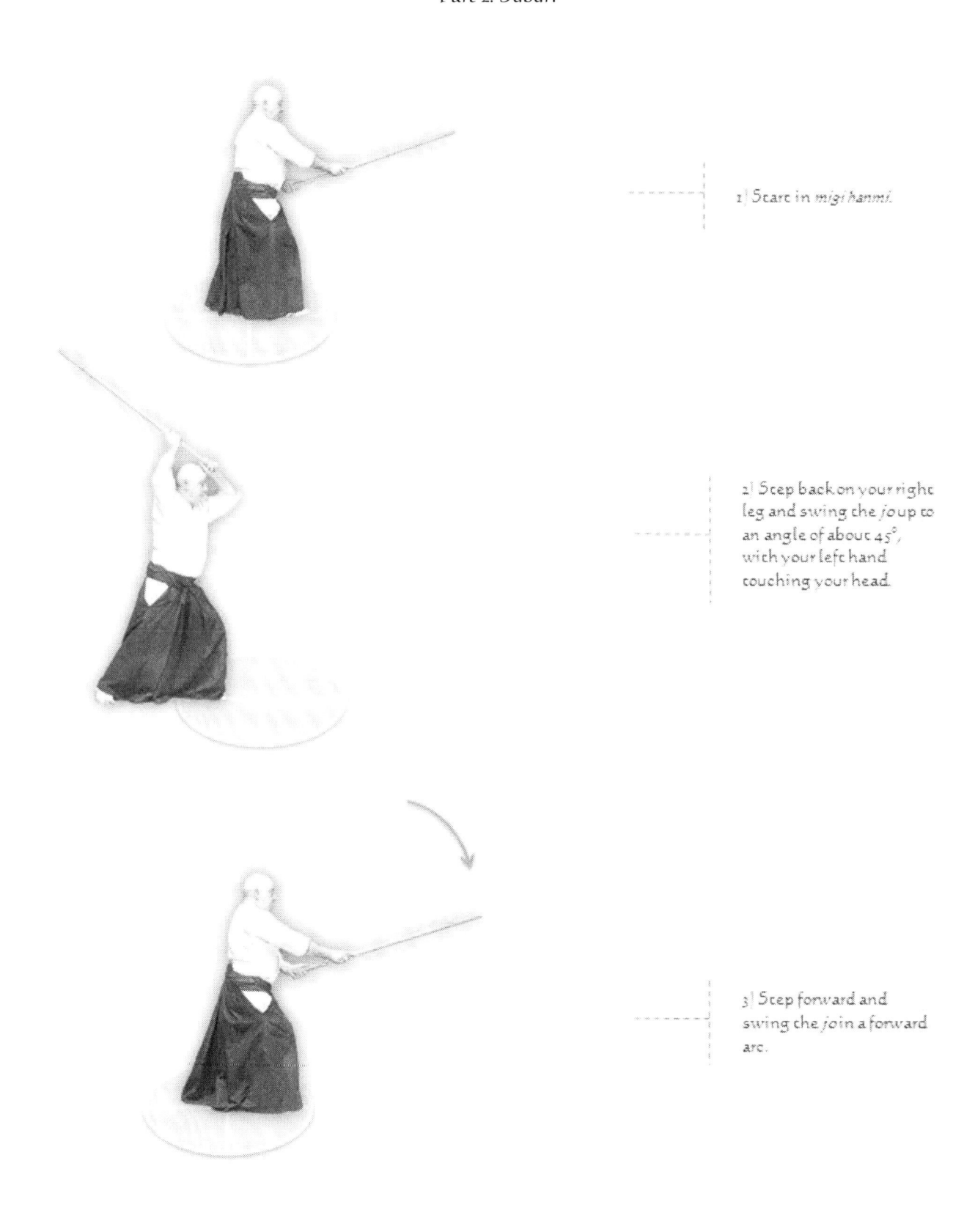

Part 2: Suburi

1| Start in *migi hanmi*.

2| Step back on your right leg and swing the *jo* up to an angle of about 45°, with your left hand touching your head.

3| Step forward and swing the *jo* in a forward arc.

[17]

Shomen uchikomi #2

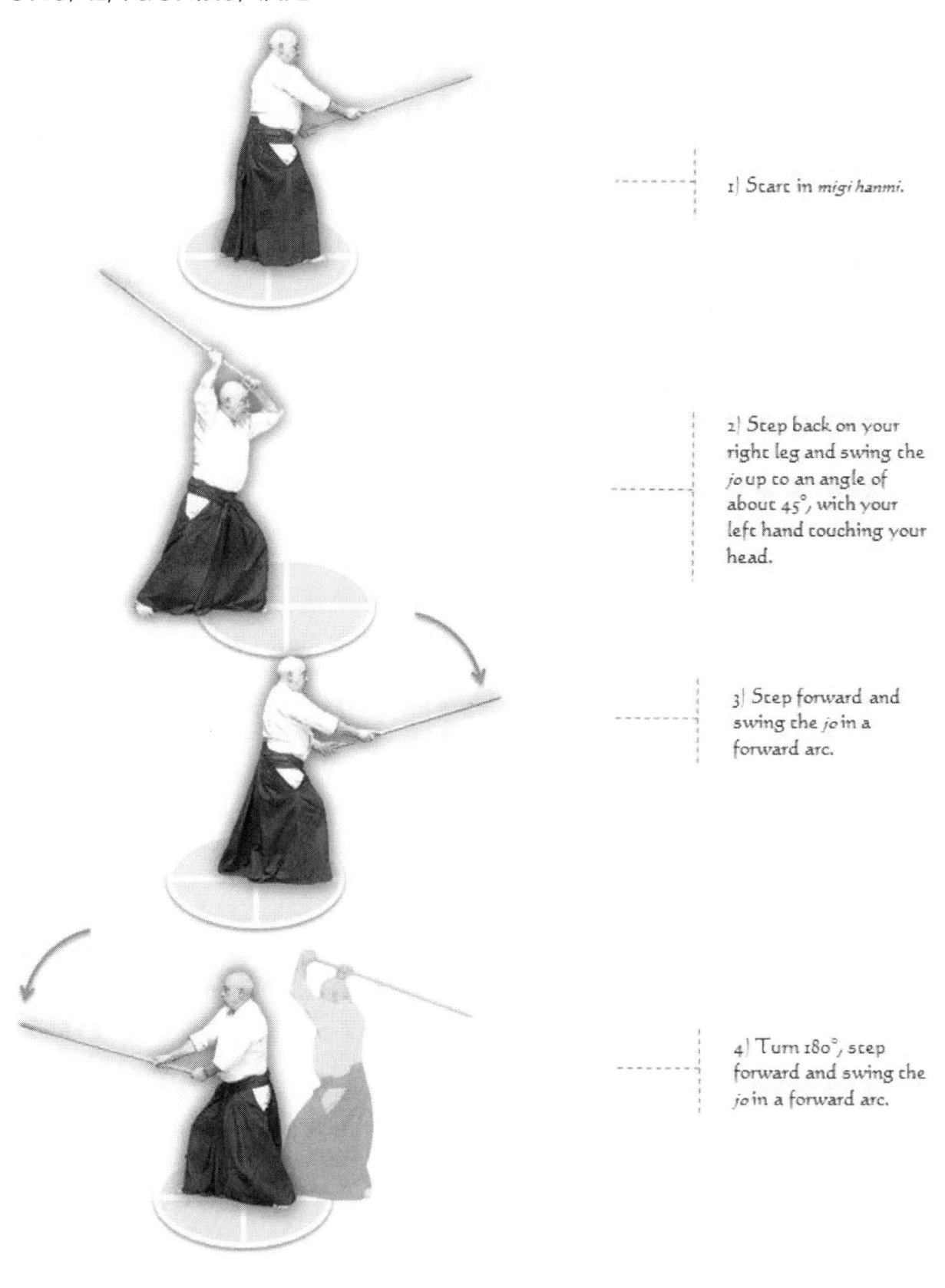

1) Start in *migi hanmi*.

2) Step back on your right leg and swing the *jo* up to an angle of about 45°, with your left hand touching your head.

3) Step forward and swing the *jo* in a forward arc.

4) Turn 180°, step forward and swing the *jo* in a forward arc.

Gyaku yokomen uchi

1) From *migi hanmi*

2) Lift your right hand to your head.

3) Step forward and to the side on your left leg, swing your arms to the right, move your weight to your left leg and swing your right leg behind your left leg.

YOKO GEDAN GAESHI

1) Stand in *hidari hanmi*

2) Swing the bottom end of the *jo* into your right hand.

3) Lift the *jo* to the left side of your head. Bring your right foot forward to your left foot, release the *jo* with your left hand so that it swings behind you, take hold of the end of the *jo* above your head with your right hand…

4) …and step back on your left leg as you swing the *jo* to *gedan* level, assuming a low posture as you do so.

CHOKU TSUKI GEDAN GAESHI

Part 2: Suburi

1) Stand in *hidari hanmi*

2) Swing the lower end of the *jo* into your right hand.

3) Lift your right arm to about head height.

4) As you step forward (*okuri ashi*) swing the *jo* to the horizontal and slide it forwards and through your left hand. Your hands rotate so that the heel of your left hand faces downwards. You finish with your front knee bent and back leg straight.

5) Slide your left hand to the end of the *jo*. Slide the *jo* back through your right hand.

6) Step forward and swing the *jo* in a forward arc at lower leg level.

Toma katate uchi

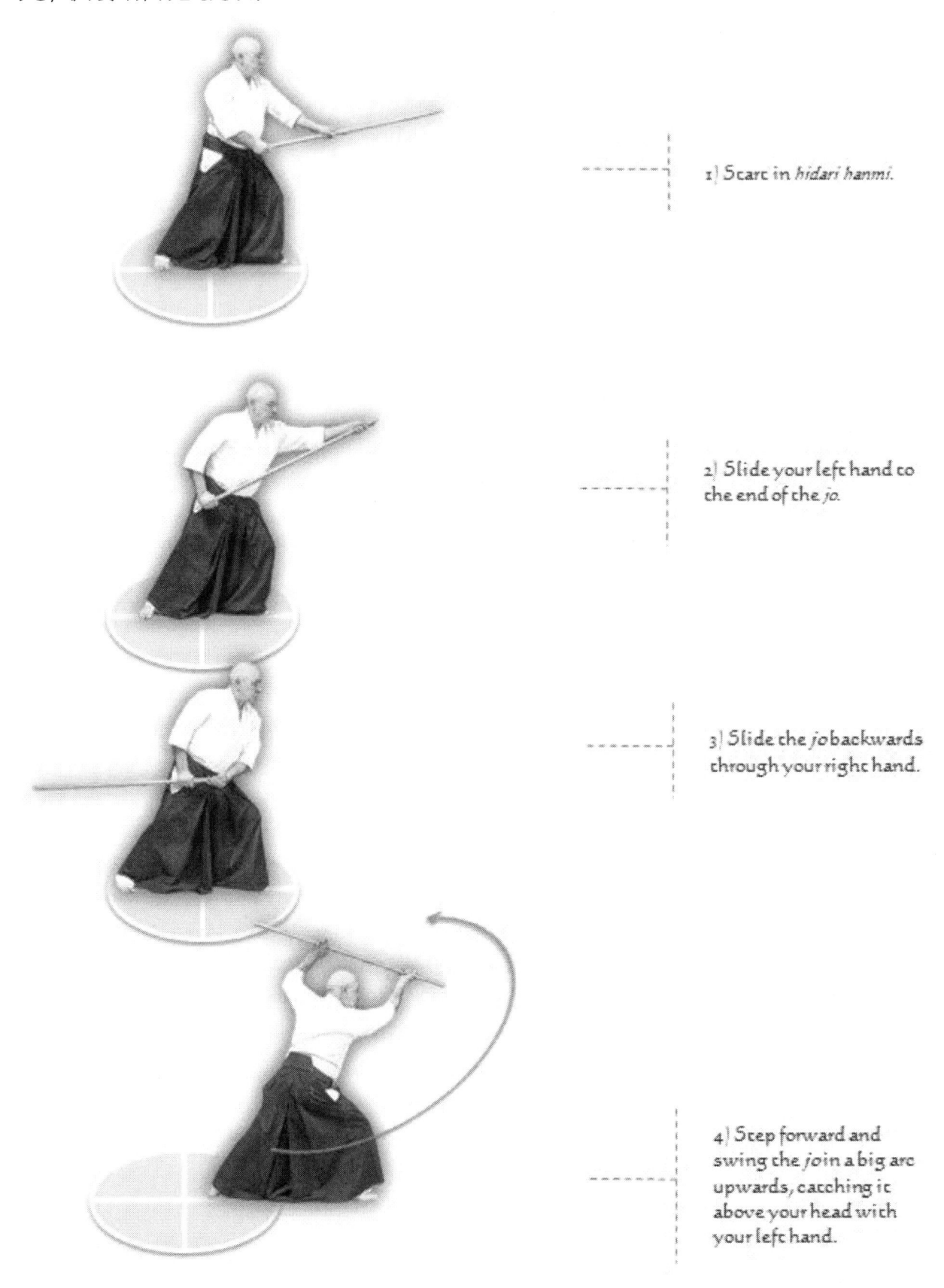

1) Start in *hidari hanmi*.

2) Slide your left hand to the end of the *jo*.

3) Slide the *jo* backwards through your right hand.

4) Step forward and swing the *jo* in a big arc upwards, catching it above your head with your left hand.

TOMA KATATE GEDAN GAESHI

1| Start in *hidari hanmi*.

2| Lift your right hand above your right shoulder and allow the *jo* to slide through your left hand.

3| Step diagonally forward on your right leg and swing the *jo* in a big downward arc with your right hand, adjusting the position of your left leg as the *jo* is swinging forward to *gedan* level.

Hasso gaeshi

1) Start in *migi hanmi*.

2) Slide your right hand towards the far end of the *jo* and lift your left hand to about head height. Step back as you swing the top end of the *jo* in a forward arc and raise your right hand to head height.

3) Bring your left hand to your right shoulder and assume the *hasso* position.

Irimi tenkan hasso gaeshi

1) Start in *migi hanmi*.

2) Slide your right hand towards the far end of the *jo* and lift your left hand to about head height as you step forward on your left leg.

3) Turn 180° clockwise.

4) Step back on your right leg and swing the top end of the *jo* in a vertical forward arc to end in the *hasso* position with your left hand just to right side of your neck.

Hasso gaeshi shomen uchi

Part 2: Suburi

1) Start in *migi hanmi*.

2) Slide your right hand towards the far end of the *jo* and lift your left hand to about head height. Step back as you swing the top end of the *jo* in a forward arc and raise your right hand to head height.

3) Bring your left hand to your right shoulder and assume the *hasso* position.

4) Change your right hand grip, move your left hand to the top of your head and swing the *jo* in a forward arc (*shomen uchi*) as you step forward.

Part 2: Suburi

Hasso ushiro gaeshi

1) Start in *hasso*.

2) Turn clockwise 180° and move the *jo* to the left side of your head.

3) Step back on your right leg and swing the *jo* in a big downward arc.

Hasso gaeshi ushiro uchi

1) Starting in *migi hanmi*, step back and assume the *hasso* position.

2) Turn 180° clockwise and...

3) ...swing the *jo* in a diagonal arc.

Hasso ushiro tsuki

1) Start in *hasso*.

2) Lower the *jo* so that you can take hold of the top end with your left hand.

3) Slide back and thrust the *jo* to your rear.

HACHI NO JI

1) From *hidari hanmi* step forward and swing the bottom end of the *jo* up and forward.

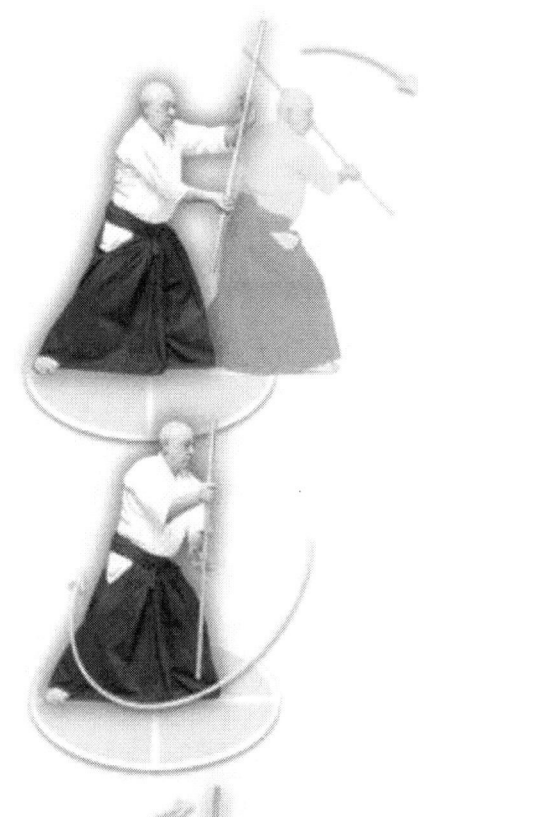

3) Swing the end of the *jo* down and towards you, then away from you again in a big forward arc as you step back.

4) The end of the *jo* swings down and to your rear and you...

5) ...align it vertically at shoulder height to the right of your head. This is termed the *hasso* position.

HACHI NO JI USHIRO TSUKI

Part 2: Suburi

1) From *hidari hanmi* step forward and swing the bottom end of the *jo* up and forward in a big arc.

3) Swing the end of the *jo* down and towards you…

4) …then away from you again in a big forward arc that brings the *jo* under your right arm.

5) Move your left hand to the end of the *jo*, step back and thrust the *jo* to your rear.

Part 3: Kata

Kata are performed at a speed that allows you to pay acute attention to the details of each movement in a series of movements. The individual movements flow together to form a continuous sequence, in the performance of which you sustain a state of calm concentration.

When performing these *kata* it is important to visualise the context of each movement, that is, what your imaginary opponent is attempting because certain movements can be interpreted as both attack and defensive manoeuvres. This ambiguity can sometimes account for *kata* being performed in slightly different ways. However, the value of performing these *kata*, that is the almost meditative rehearsal of key *suburi*, is not lost whatever the precise form practised.

Part 3: Kata

Nana no kata (7 count kata)

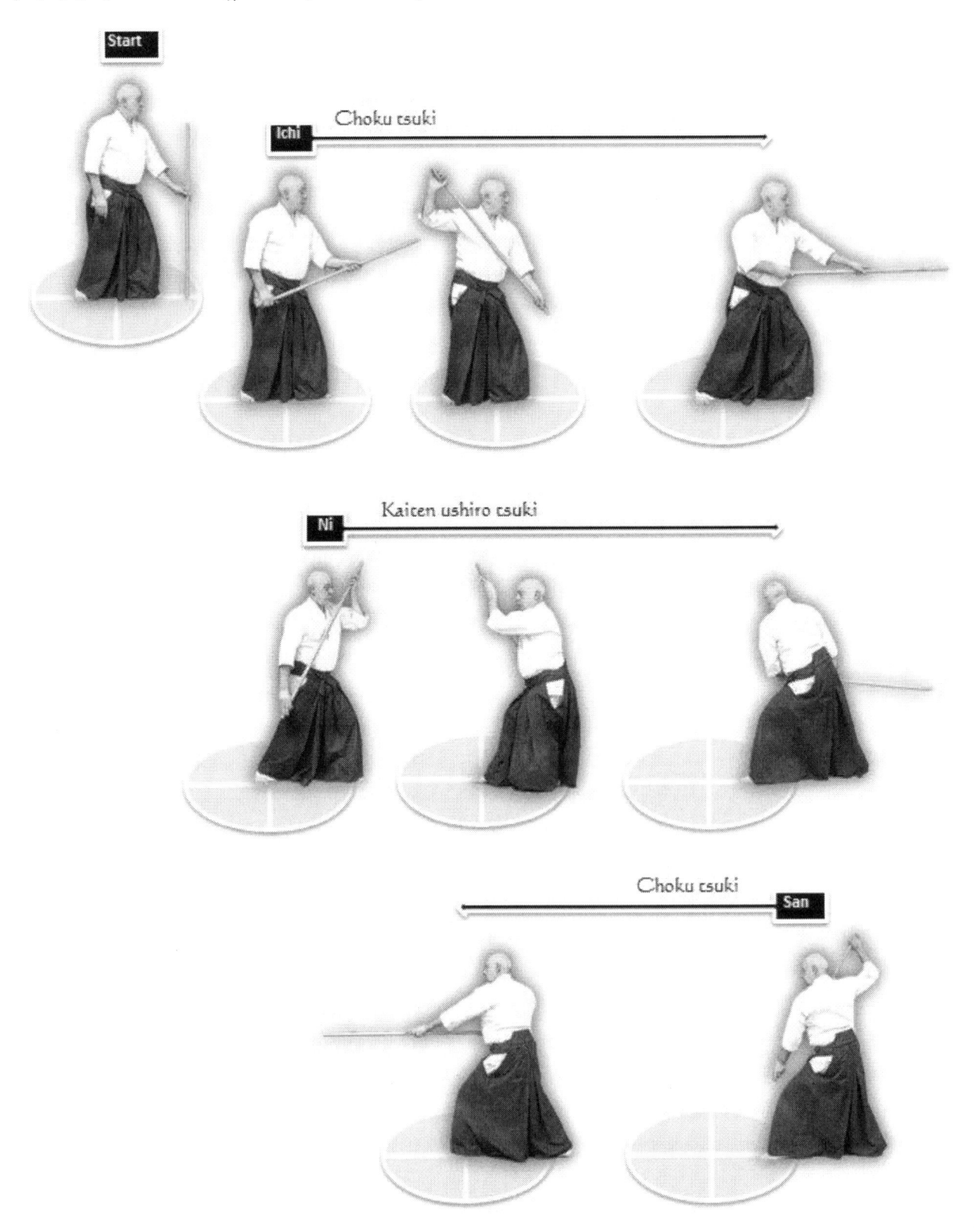

Start

Ichi — Choku tsuki

Ni — Kaiten ushiro tsuki

Choku tsuki — San

[34]

Nana no kata… cont.

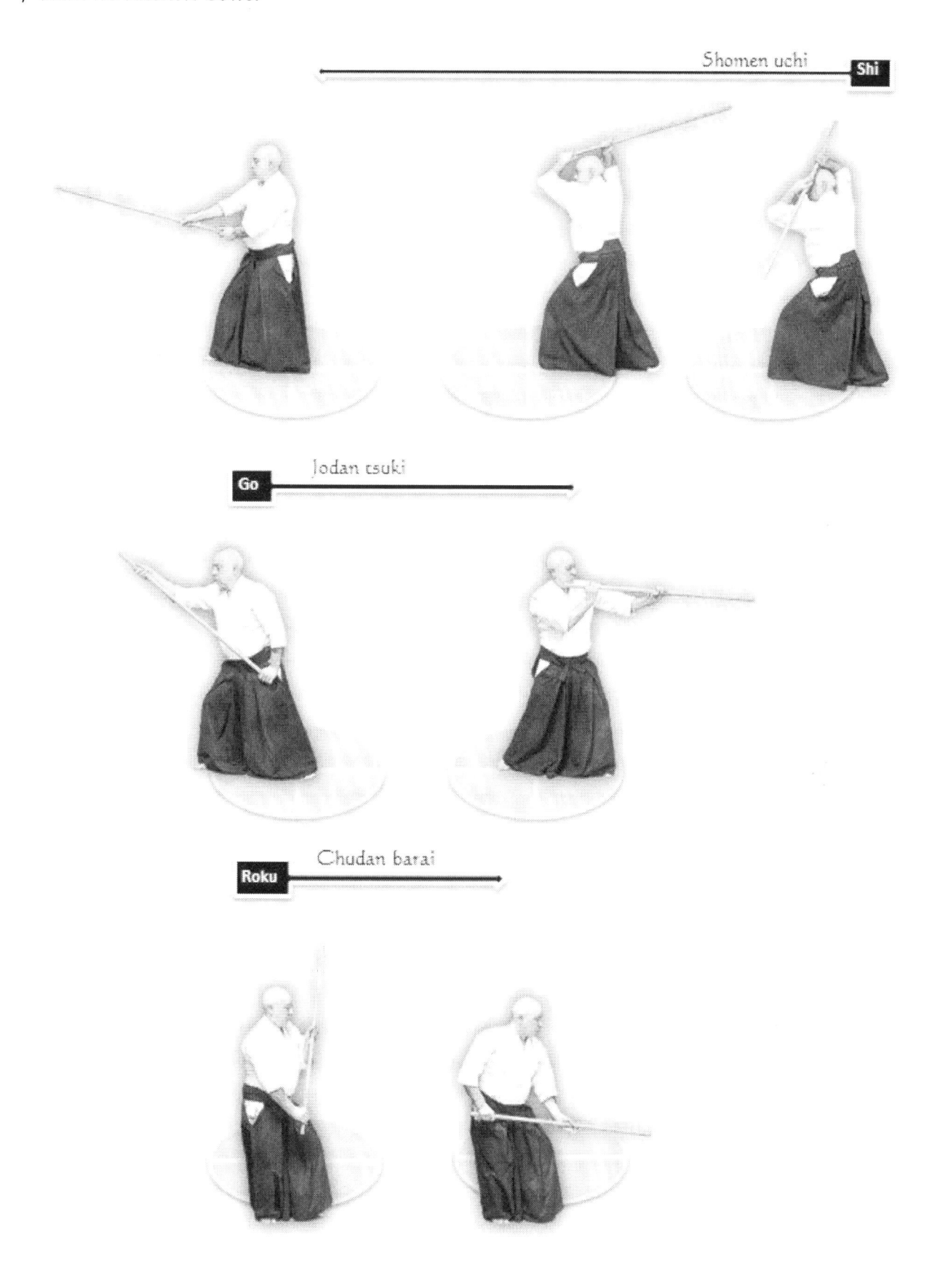

Shomen uchi — Shi

Go — Jodan tsuki

Roku — Chudan barai

Nana no kata... cont.

Shichi — Choku tsuki

Finish

Ju san no kata (13 count kata)

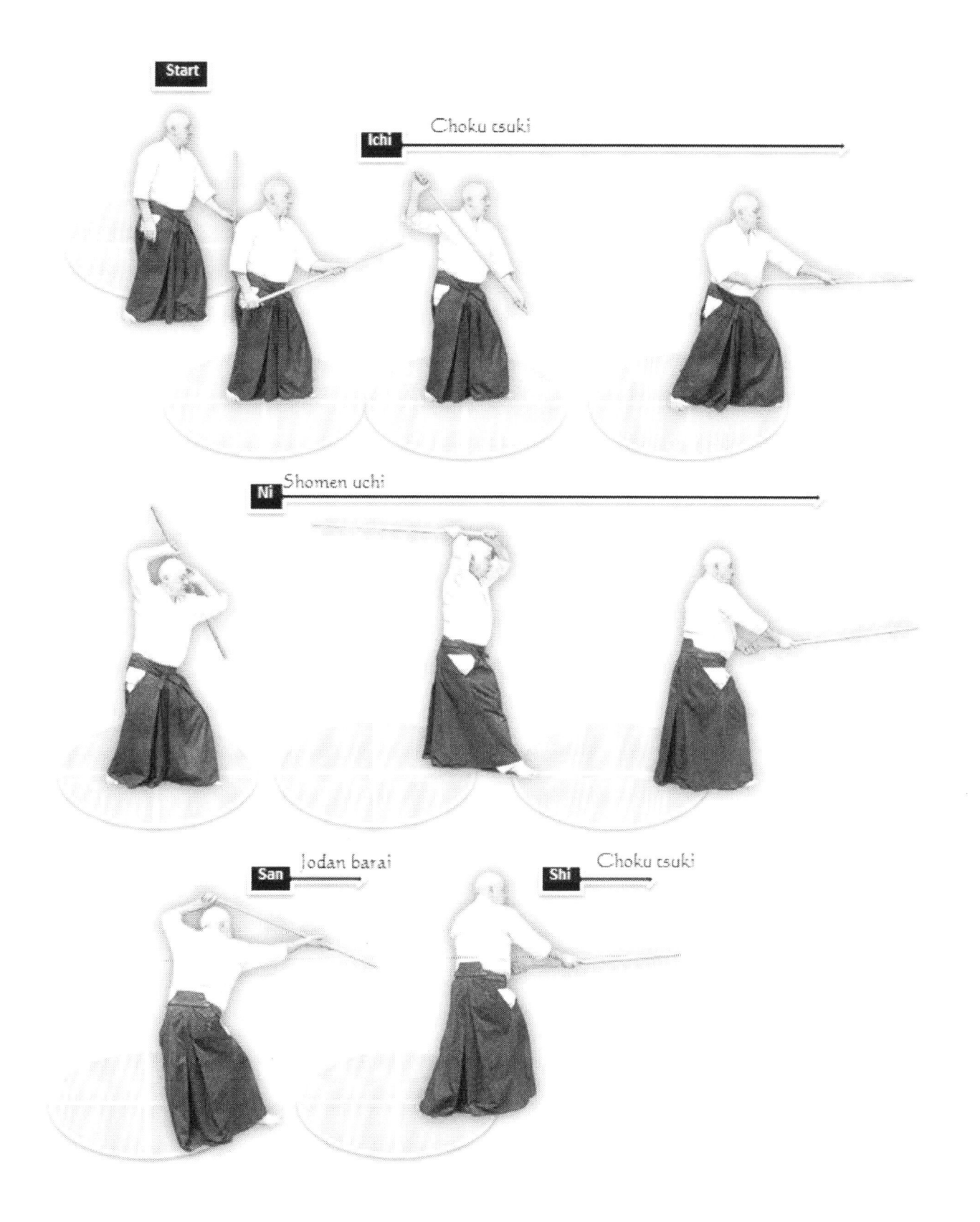

Ju san no kata… cont.

Tenkan hasso gaeshi — **Go**

Yokomen uchi — **Roku**

Shichi — Yoko barai

Hachi — Choku tsuki

Ju san no kata... cont.

Ku — Ushiro tsuki

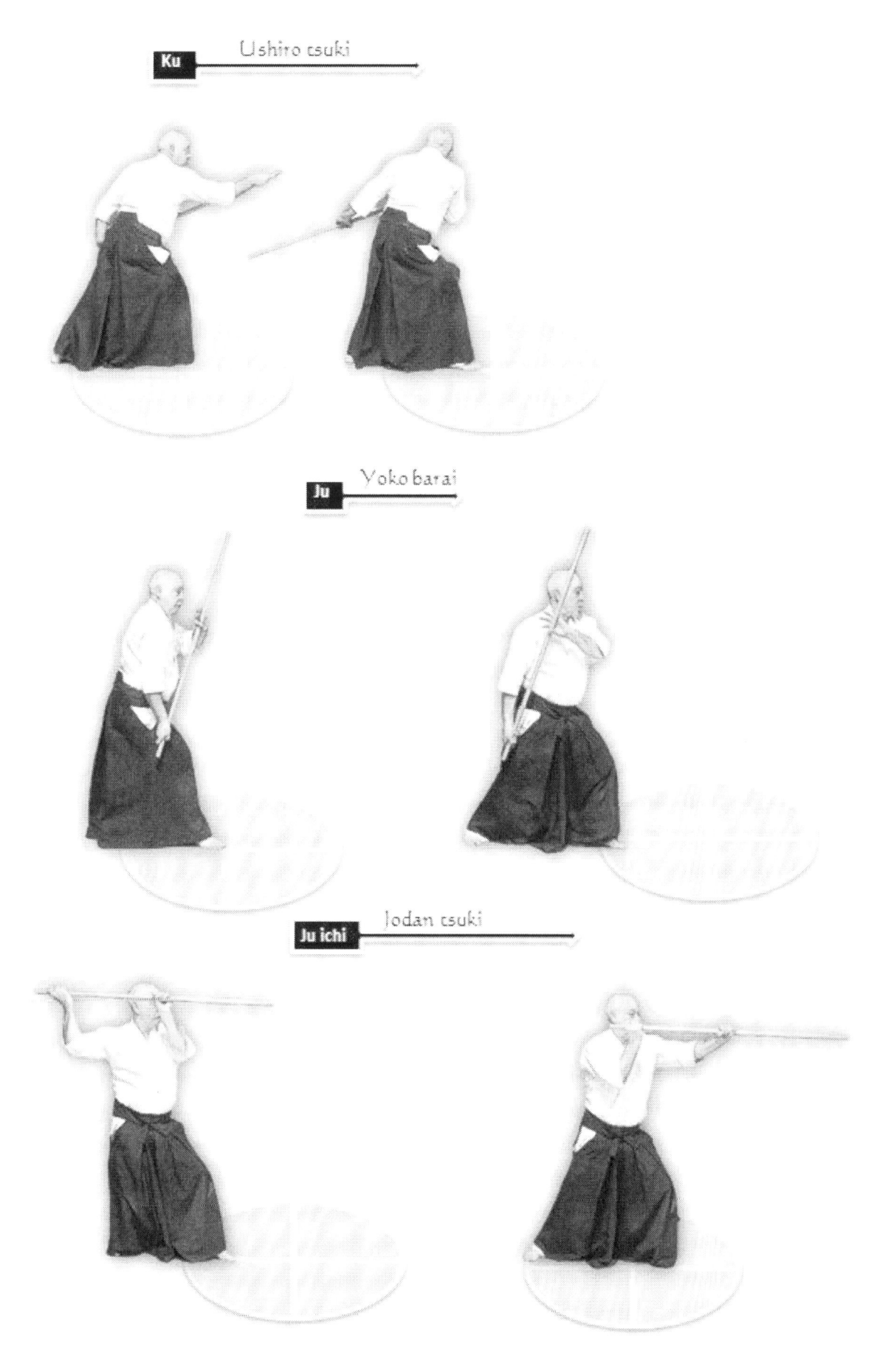

Ju — Yoko barai

Ju ichi — Jodan tsuki

Ju san no kata... cont.

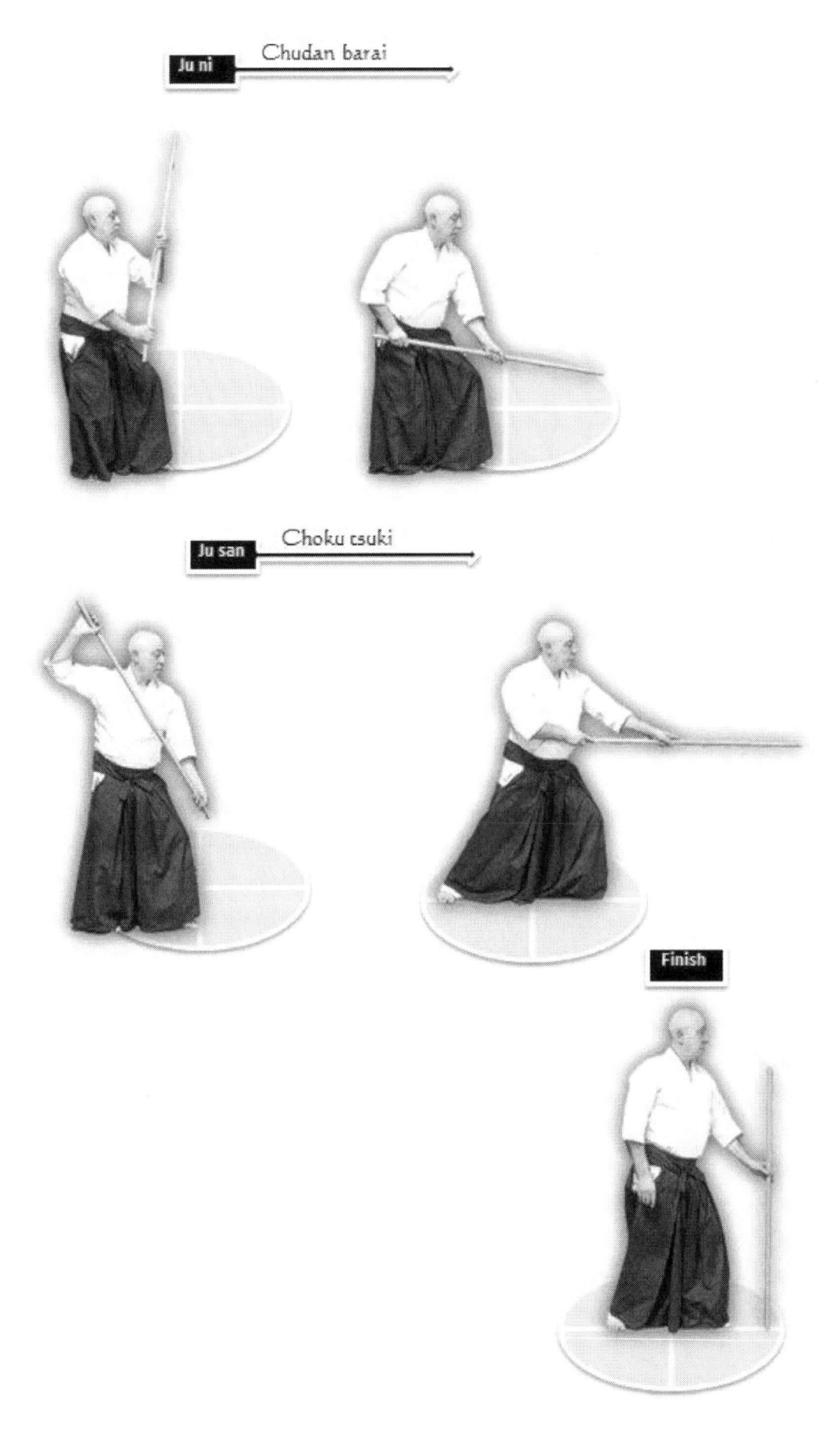

Ju ni — Chudan barai

Ju san — Choku tsuki

Finish

Part 3: Kata

San Ju Ichi No Kata (31 Count Kata)

Start

Ichi — Kaeshi tsuki

Ni — Jodan barai

San — Choku tsuki

Shi — Jodan barai

Go — Shomen uchi

San ju ichi no kata... cont.

Roku — Gyaku shomen uchi

Shichi — Shomen uchi

Hachi — Gyaku shomen uchi

San ju ichi no kata... cont.

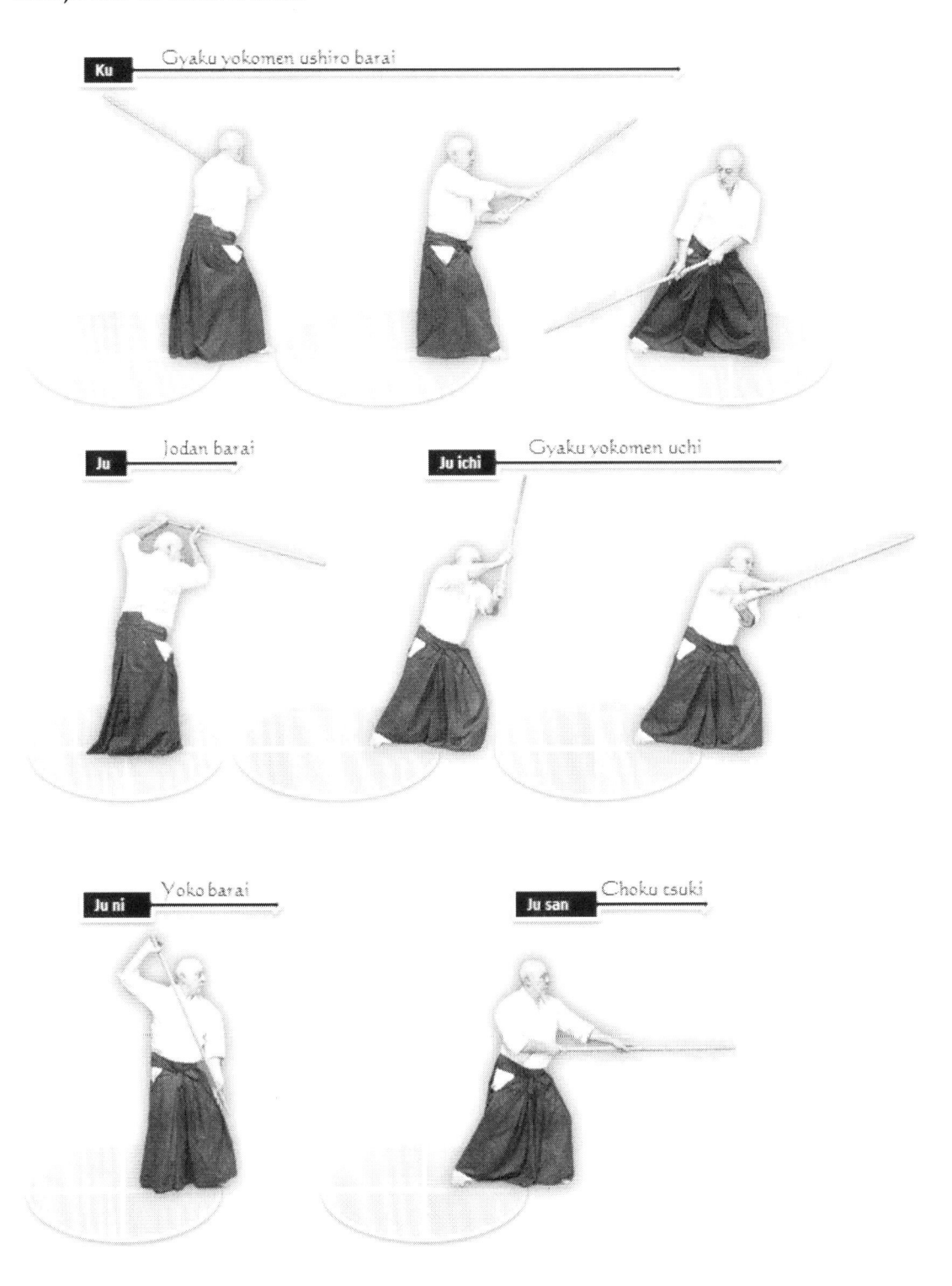

Ku — Gyaku yokomen ushiro barai

Ju — Jodan barai

Ju ichi — Gyaku yokomen uchi

Ju ni — Yoko barai

Ju san — Choku tsuki

San ju ichi no kata... cont.

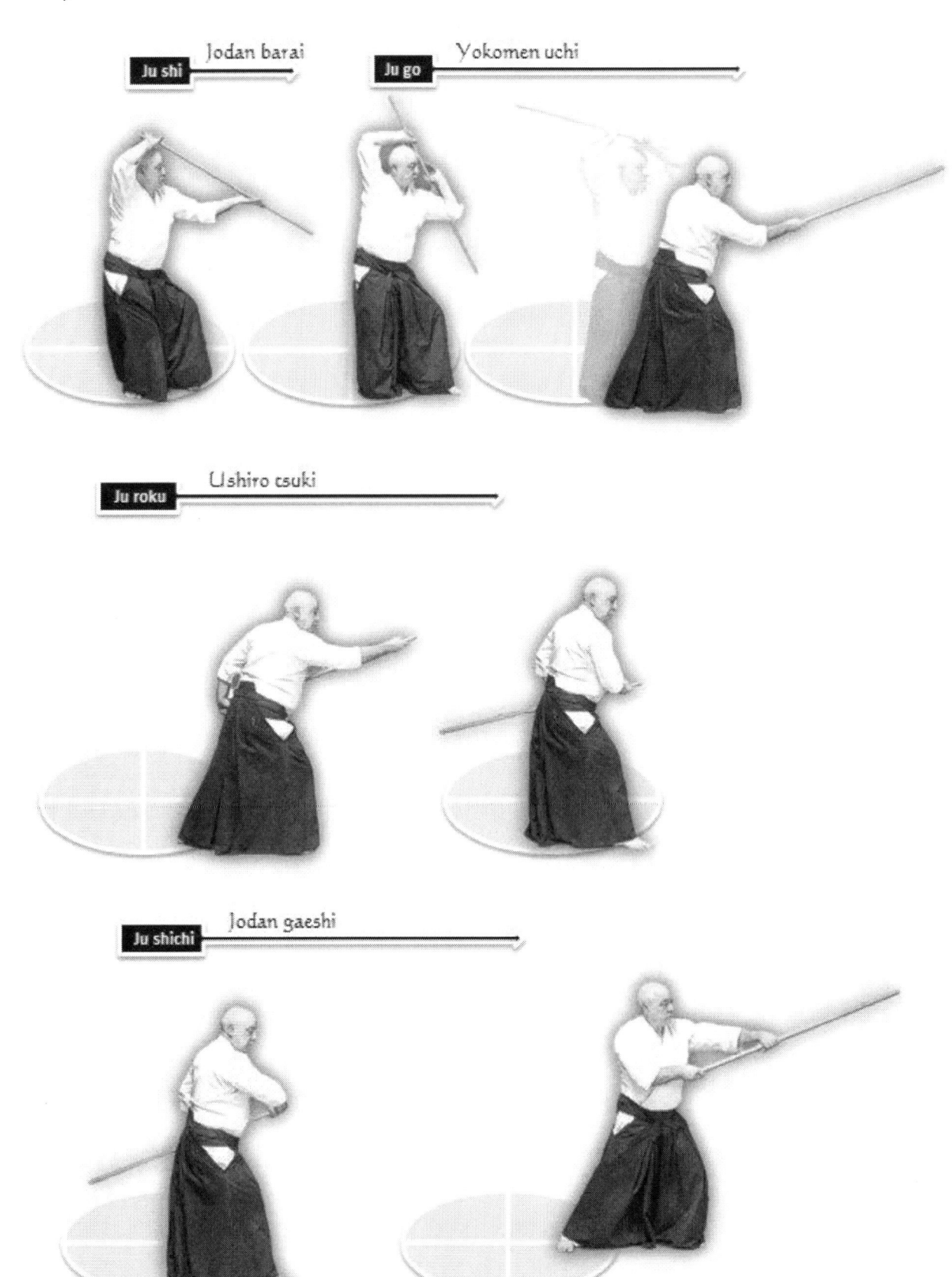

Ju shi — Jodan barai

Ju go — Yokomen uchi

Ju roku — Ushiro csuki

Ju shichi — Jodan gaeshi

San ju ichi no kata… cont.

Ju hachi — Chudan barai

Ju ku — Choku tsuki

Ni ju — Gedan gaeshi

San ju ichi no kata… cont.

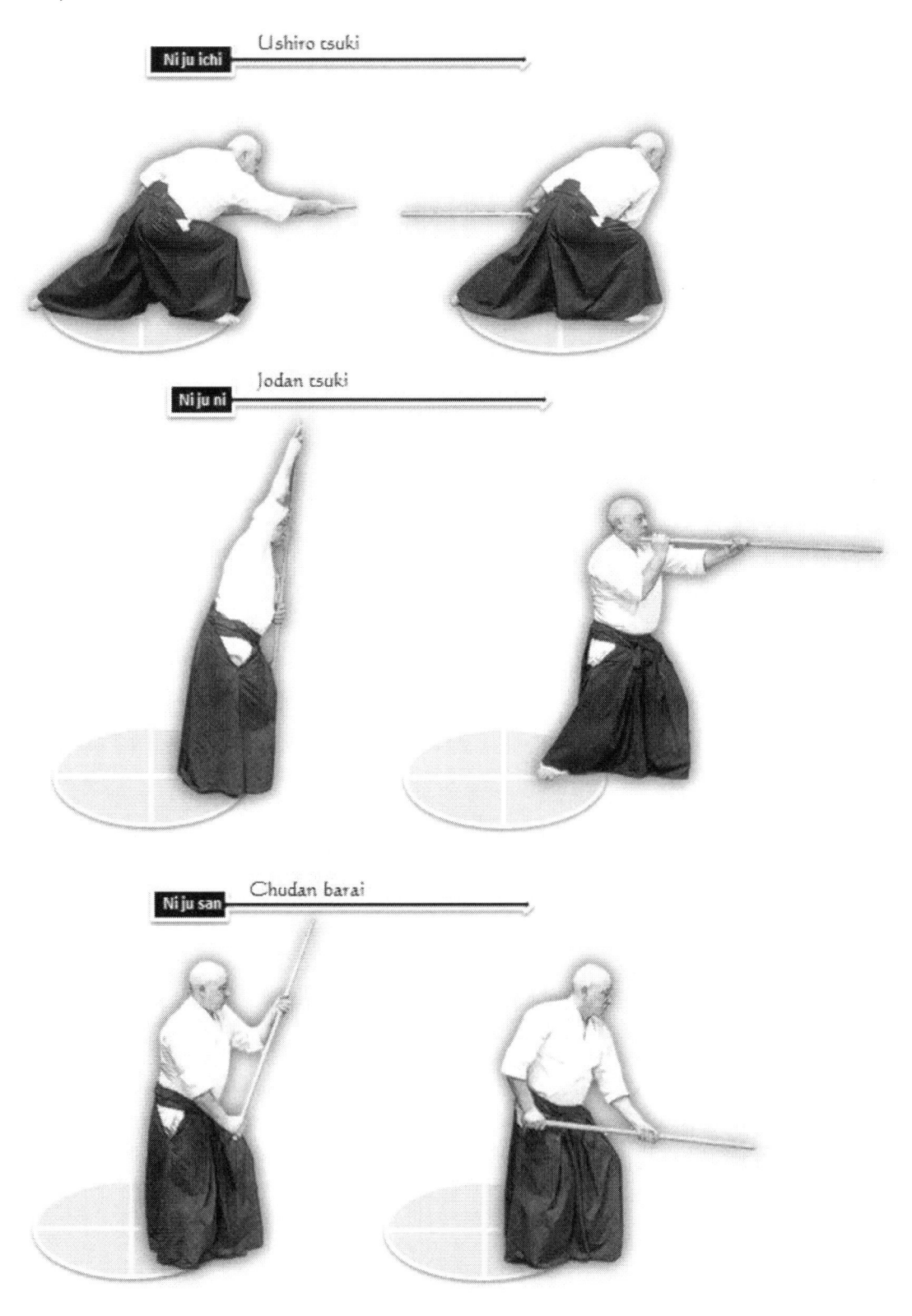

Ni ju ichi — Ushiro tsuki

Ni ju ni — Jodan tsuki

Ni ju san — Chudan barai

San ju ichi no kata... cont.

Ni ju shi — Choku tsuki

Ni ju go — Jodan tsuki

Ni ju roku — Ushiro tsuki

Part 3: Kata

San ju ichi no kata... cont.

Ni ju shichi — Gedan gaeshi

Ni ju hachi — Jodan tsuki

Ni ju ku — Chudan barai

San ju — Choku tsuki

San ju ichi — Gyaku yokomen uchi

Finish

[48]

Part 4: Jo dori

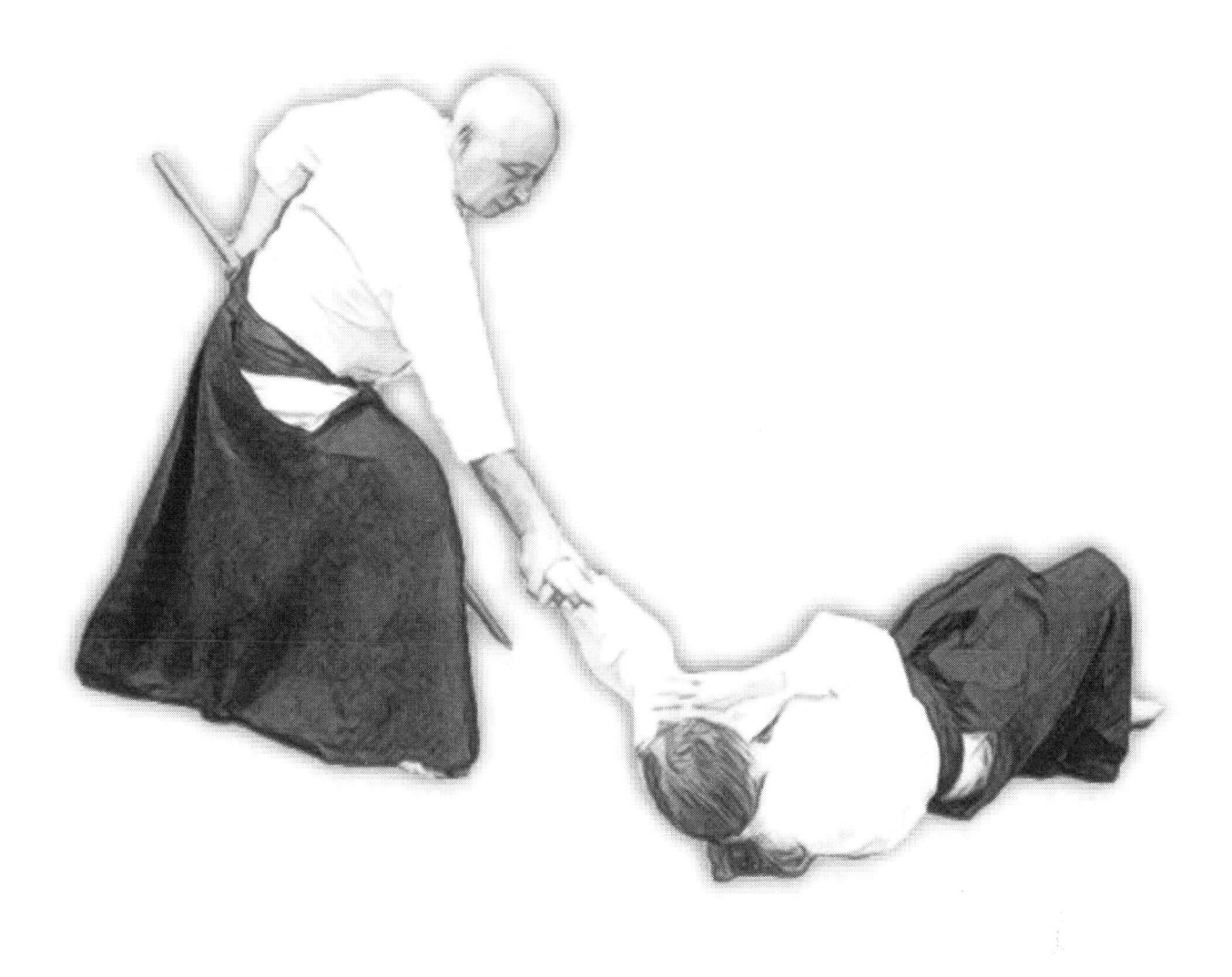

In *jo dori*, *uke* is attempting to strike you with the *jo*. You move off the line of attack and either use the *jo* to throw or pin *uke*. This form of practice adds an element of danger and requires you to move quickly and to control *uke* in mechanically efficient ways.

Kokyu nage #1

1) *Uke* attacks with *choku tsuki*.

2) Moving to your left you take hold of the *jo* with both hands.

3) You lift the end of the *jo* in your right hand, making your left hand a pivot point.

4) Turning to your right you extend the lower end of the *jo* under *uke's* left arm.

5) Finally you extend the *jo* down and to *uke's* rear, causing her to lose balance and fall.

Kokyu nage #2

Part 4: Jo dori

1) *Uke* attacks with *choku tsuki*.

2) Moving to your left you take hold of the *jo* with both hands.

3) You lower the end of the *jo* in your right hand, making your left hand a pivot point.

4) Turning to your right you extend the upper end of the *jo* forward and down causing *uke* to lose balance and fall.

Part 4: Jo dori

KOKYU NAGE #3

1) *Uke* attacks with *choku tsuki*.

2) Moving to your left you take hold of the *jo* with both hands.

3) You lower the end of the *jo* in your right hand and turn to your left.

4) Moving forward on your left leg, you extend the upper end of the *jo* forward and down causing *uke* to lose balance and fall.

Part 4: Jo dori

Kokyu nage #4

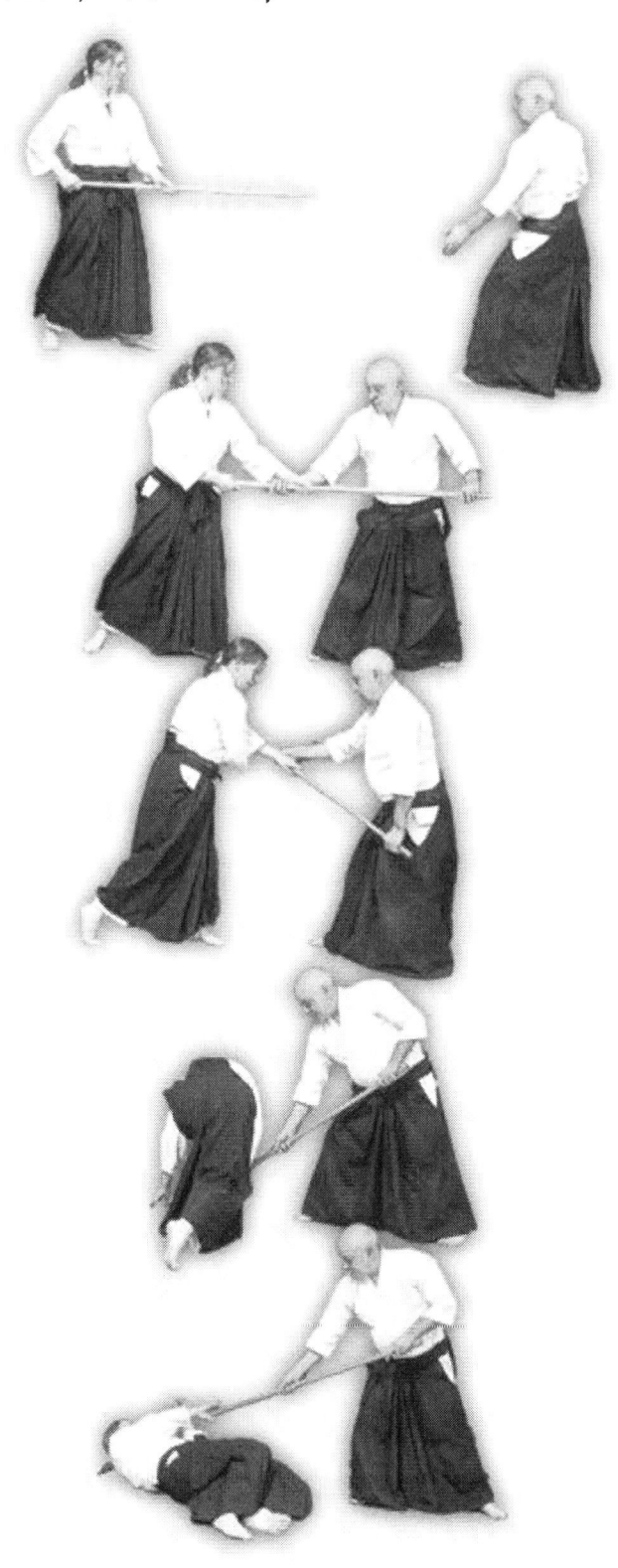

1) *Uke* attacks with *choku tsuki*.

2) Moving to your right you take hold of the *jo* with both hands.

3) You turn to your right and extend the end of the *jo* in your left hand outwards so that the other end of the *jo* moves between you and *uke*.

4) Moving forward on your right leg, you extend the *jo* forward and down causing *uke* to lose balance and fall.

Part 4: Jo dori

KOKYU NAGE #5

1) *Uke* attacks with *choku tsuki*.

2) Moving to your left you take hold of the *jo* with both hands.

3) You step forward and turn 180° to your left, dropping the end of the *jo* in your right hand so that the other end extends *uke* forward and off-balance.

4) You hook *uke's* left leg at the knee and rotate the *jo* so the the lower end swings forward as the other end swings backwards, throwing *uke* to the mat.

Kokyu nage #6

1) *Uke* attacks with *choku tsuki*.

2) Stepping to your right you take hold of the *jo* with both hands and pivot on your front (right) leg so you are at about 90° to the line of *uke's* attack.

4) Moving forward on your right leg, you extend the *jo* forward and down causing *uke* to lose balance and fall.

Kote gaeshi

1) *Uke* attacks with *choku tsuki*.

2) Stepping to your right you turn and drop your hand on to the back of *uke's* leading hand.

3) Turning to your right you swing the *jo* up and to your right, using your left hand to establish the *Kote gaeshi* control, as you step forward and throw *uke*.

Part 4: Jo dori

SHIHO NAGE

1) *Uke* attacks with *choku tsuki*.

2) Moving to your left you take hold of the *jo* with both hands.

3) You turn to your left extending the end of the *jo* in your left hand upwards, and to your left, as the other end moves between you and *uke*.

4) You step forward on your right leg, passing under uke's arms, and turn 180° to your left lifting the end of the *jo* in your right hand so that *uke* falls backwards.

Ikkyo

1) *Uke* attacks with *choku tsuki*.

2) Moving to your left you drop your left hand on to the back of *uke's* left hand.

3) Turning to your left you swing the *jo* up and to your left as you take hold of the end of the *jo* with your right hand.

4) Swinging your arms down, with the *jo* held along *uke's* left arm, you step forward and pin her, face down.

Part 5: Jo Waza

In *jo waza* you hold the *jo* and *uke* grabs it with one or both hands. You apply a throwing or locking technique in response. This form of training forces you to apply mechanically sound principles to overcome *uke's* control of the *jo*, these principles being directly relevant to unarmed *Aikido* training.

Kokyu ho #1

1) *Uke* takes hold of the *jo* with his right hand.

2) You swing the end in your right hand forward as you turn your hips to the left. The other end of the *jo* extends upwards.

3) You step under *uke's* right arm and turn 180°.

4) Stepping forward on your right leg you turn to your left and extend the *jo* across *uke's* upper body.

Kokyu ho #2

1) *Uke* takes hold of the *jo* with his right hand.

2) You step to your left (*sokumen*).

3) Extending the *jo* across *uke's* upper body you step forward on your left leg.

Kokyu nage #1

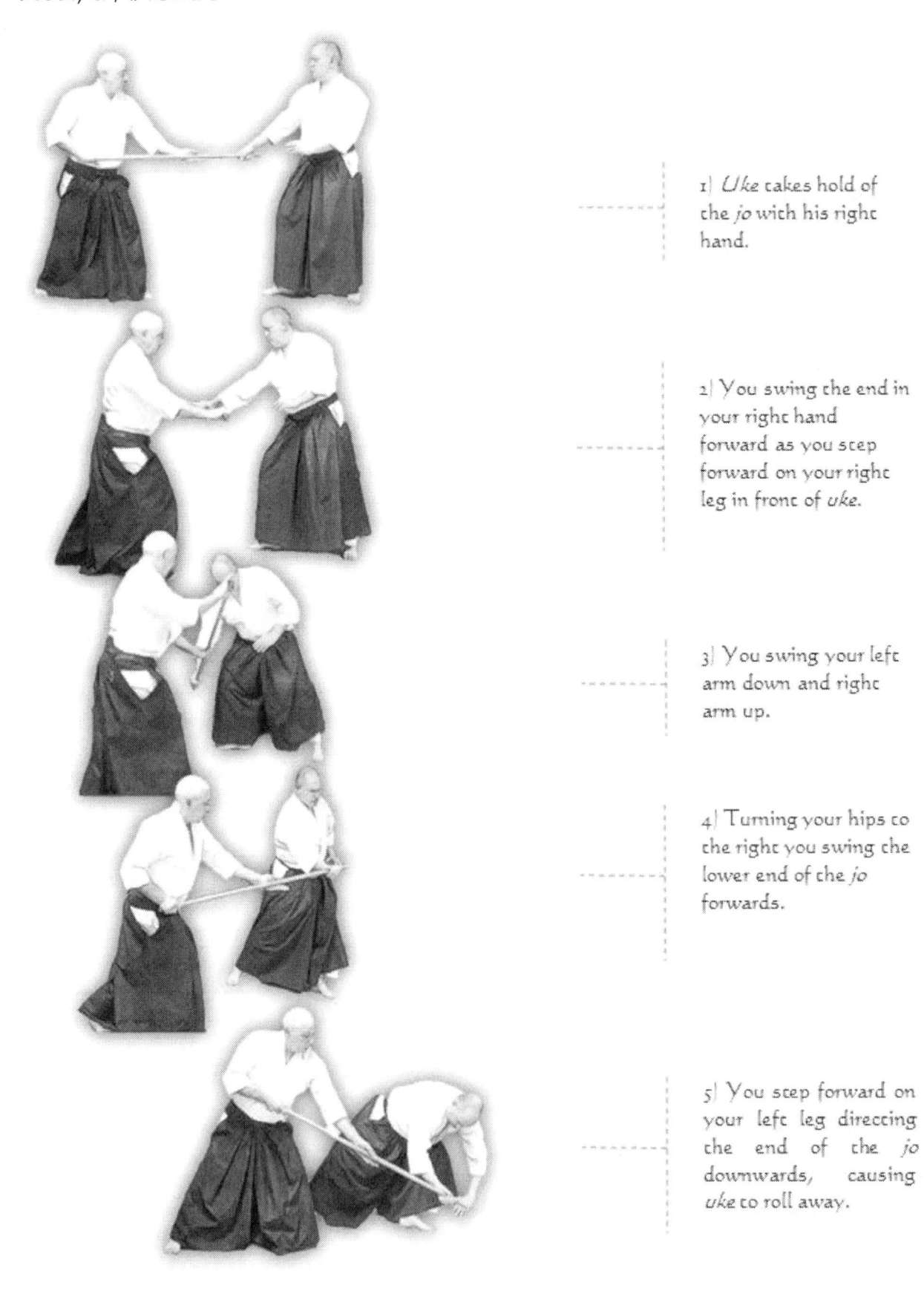

1) *Uke* takes hold of the *jo* with his right hand.

2) You swing the end in your right hand forward as you step forward on your right leg in front of *uke*.

3) You swing your left arm down and right arm up.

4) Turning your hips to the right you swing the lower end of the *jo* forwards.

5) You step forward on your left leg directing the end of the *jo* downwards, causing *uke* to roll away.

Kokyu nage #2

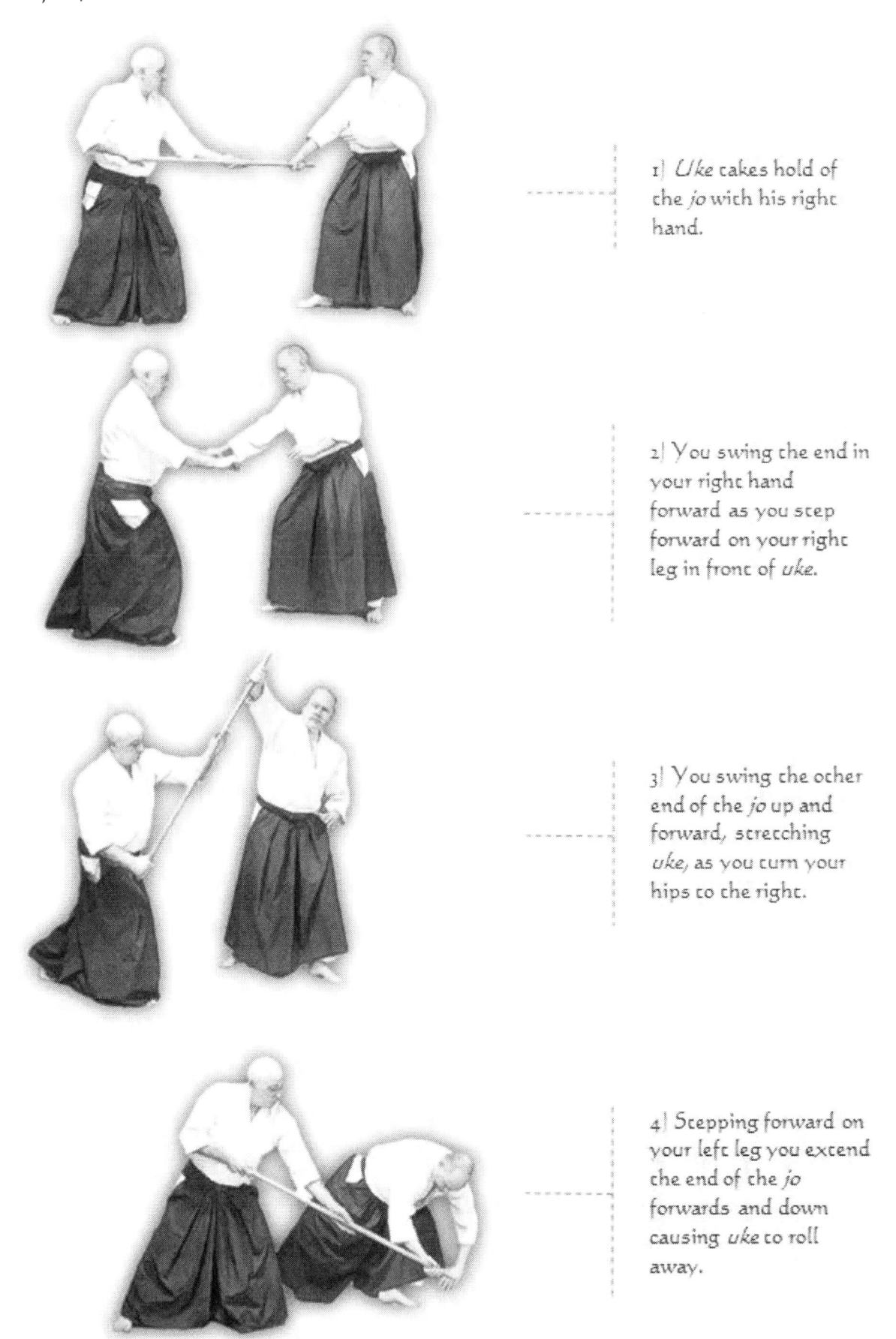

1) *Uke* takes hold of the *jo* with his right hand.

2) You swing the end in your right hand forward as you step forward on your right leg in front of *uke*.

3) You swing the other end of the *jo* up and forward, stretching *uke*, as you turn your hips to the right.

4) Stepping forward on your left leg you extend the end of the *jo* forwards and down causing *uke* to roll away.

Kokyu nage #3

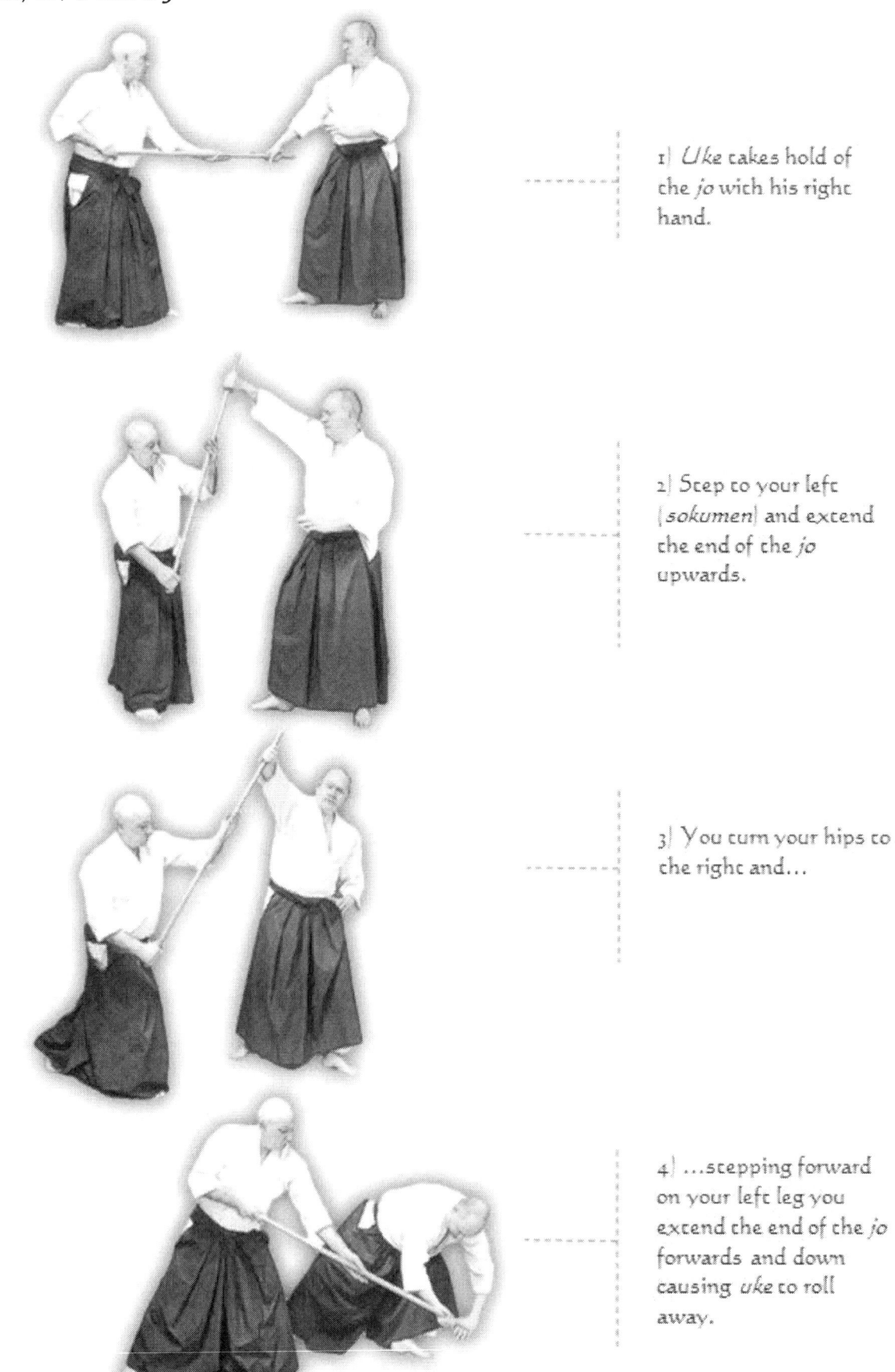

1) *Uke* takes hold of the *jo* with his right hand.

2) Step to your left (*sokumen*) and extend the end of the *jo* upwards.

3) You turn your hips to the right and…

4) …stepping forward on your left leg you extend the end of the *jo* forwards and down causing *uke* to roll away.

Kokyu nage #4

1) *Uke* takes hold of the *jo* with his right hand.

2) You turn to the right and...

3) ...step forward on your left leg as you swing the end of the *jo* upwards.

4) Turning 180° to your right and stepping forward on your left leg you extend the end of the *jo* forwards and down causing *uke* to roll away.

Kokyu nage #5

1) *Uke* takes hold of the *jo* with his right hand.

2) You swing the end of the *jo* up as you step forward to *uke's* left side.

3) Turning 180° (*kaiten*) you extend the lower end of the *jo* towards the inside of *uke's* left leg.

4) You extend the upper end of the *jo* forward and down as you hook the inside of *uke's* left leg, causing him to topple forward and fall.

Kokyu nage #6

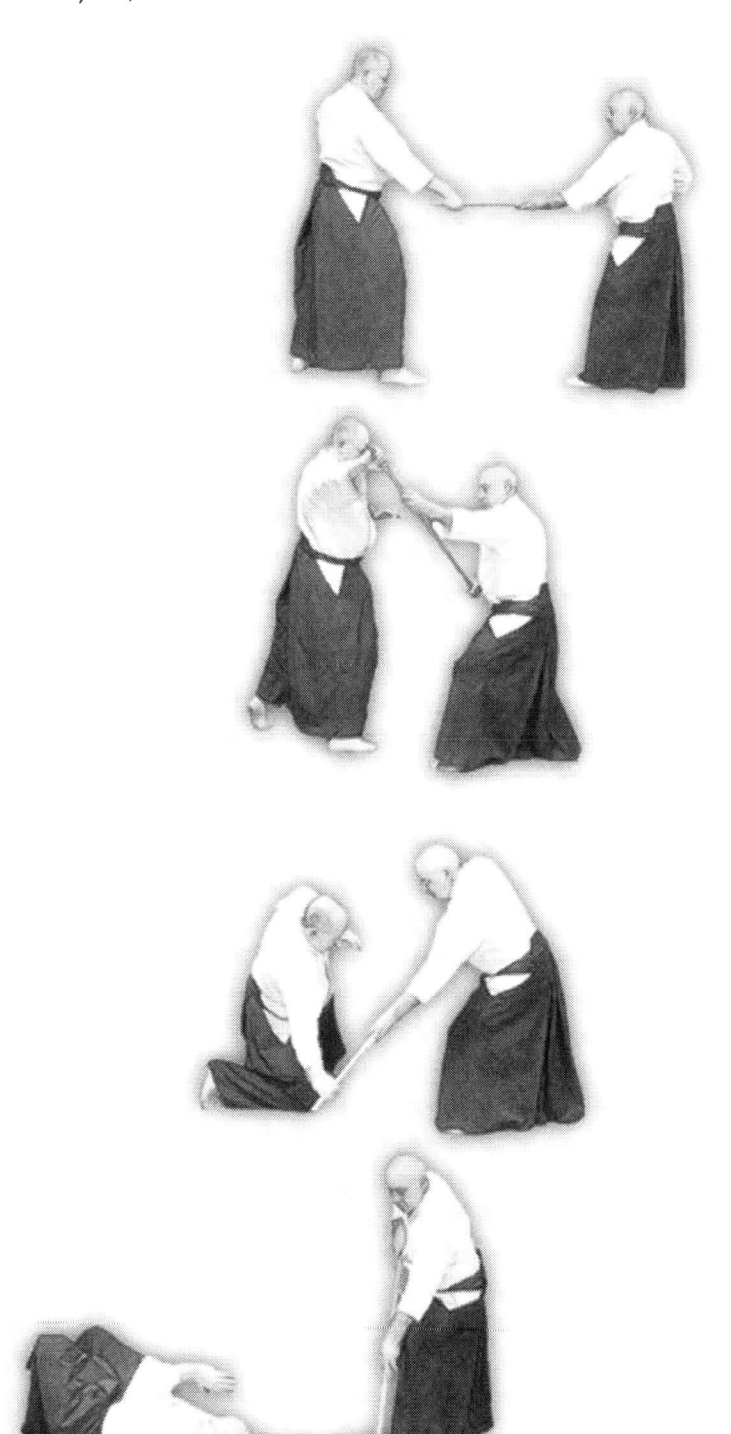

1) *Uke* takes hold of the *jo* with his right hand.

2) Moving to the side you extend the end of the *jo* up and to your left, leading *uke* on to his right leg.

3) You break *uke's* balance by extending the *jo* to the side and down..

Kokyu nage #7

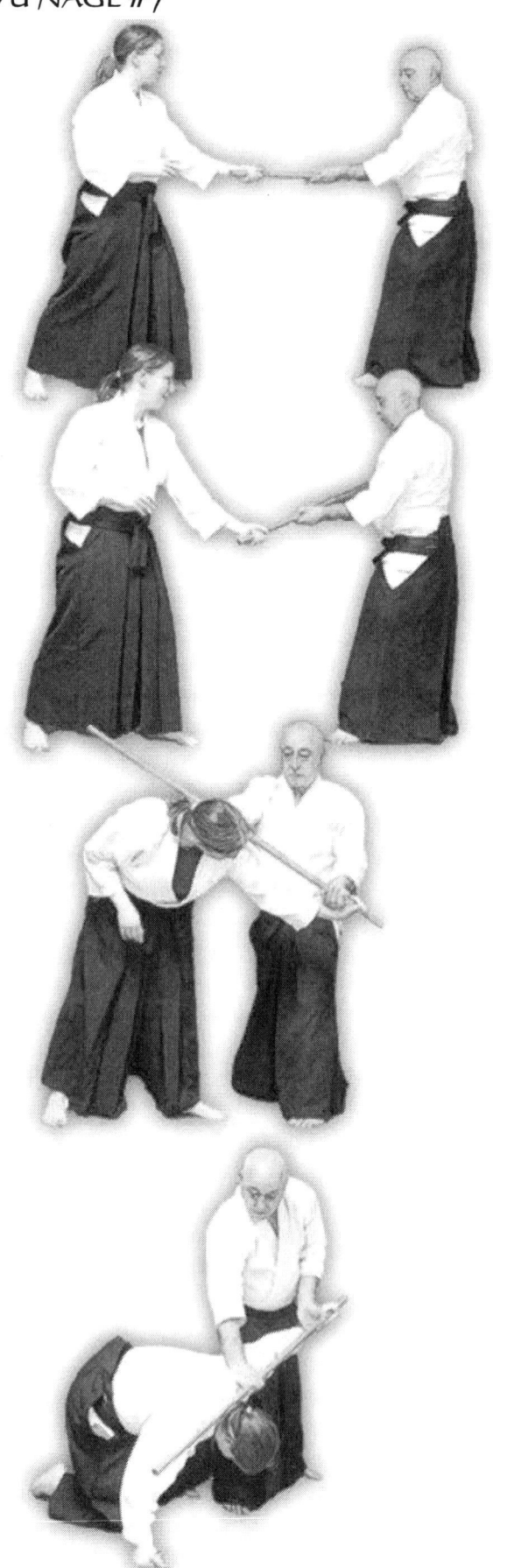

1) *Uke* takes hold of the *jo* with her left hand.

2) You swing the end in your right hand forward as you step forward on your right leg behind *uke*. Your right hand slides down to about the middle of the *jo*.

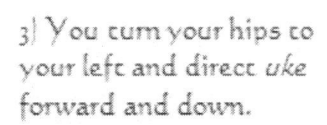

3) You turn your hips to your left and direct *uke* forward and down.

Kata gatame

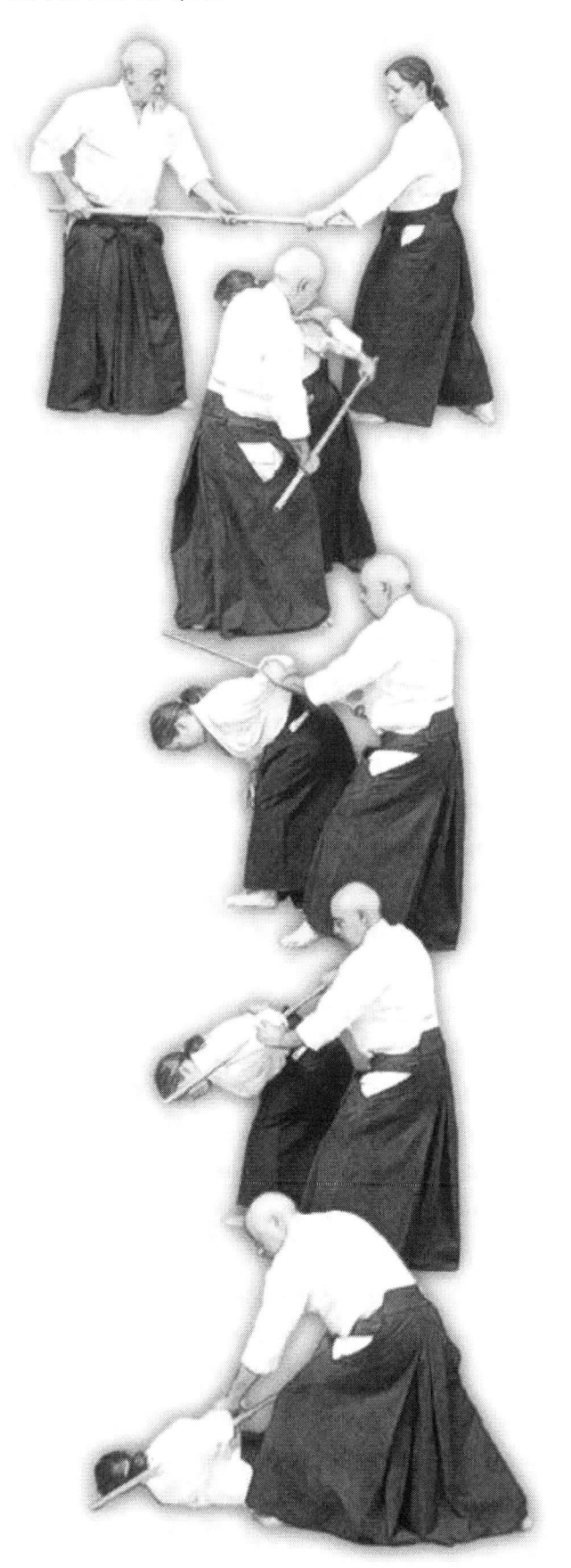

1) *Uke* takes hold of the *jo* with her left hand.

2) You step diagonally forward, extending the end of the *jo* behind *uke's* back and take hold of her left elbow with your left hand.

3) You extend the end of the *jo* up along the line of *uke's* spine.

4) You direct the end of the *jo* down across *uke's* left elbow, pinning her to the mat.

Part 5: Jo waza

Nikyo

1) *Uke* takes hold of the *jo* with his right hand.

2) You step to the side (*sokumen*) and swing the end of the *jo* up.

3) You swing *jo* down in front of you and drop your left hand on to the back of *uke's* right hand.

4) You turn to your left beding *uke's* arm at wrist and elbow. Using your left hand position as a pivot point you apply the *Nikyo* control to *uke's* right wrist.

Nikyo ... cont.

5) You direct the end of the *jo* towards *uke's* right armpit.

6) You push the end of the *jo* under *uke's* arm and...

7) ...lift the other end to pin *uke's* arm.

Sankyo

1) *Uke* takes hold of the *jo* with his right hand.

2) You step to the side (*sokumen*) and swing the end of the *jo* up.

3) You swing *jo* down in front of you take hold of the side of his right hand from underneath.

4) You use the other end of the *jo* to control to *uke's* right wrist.

5) Maintaining the *Sankyo* control with your left hand, you direct *uke* face down to the mat.

SHIHO NAGE

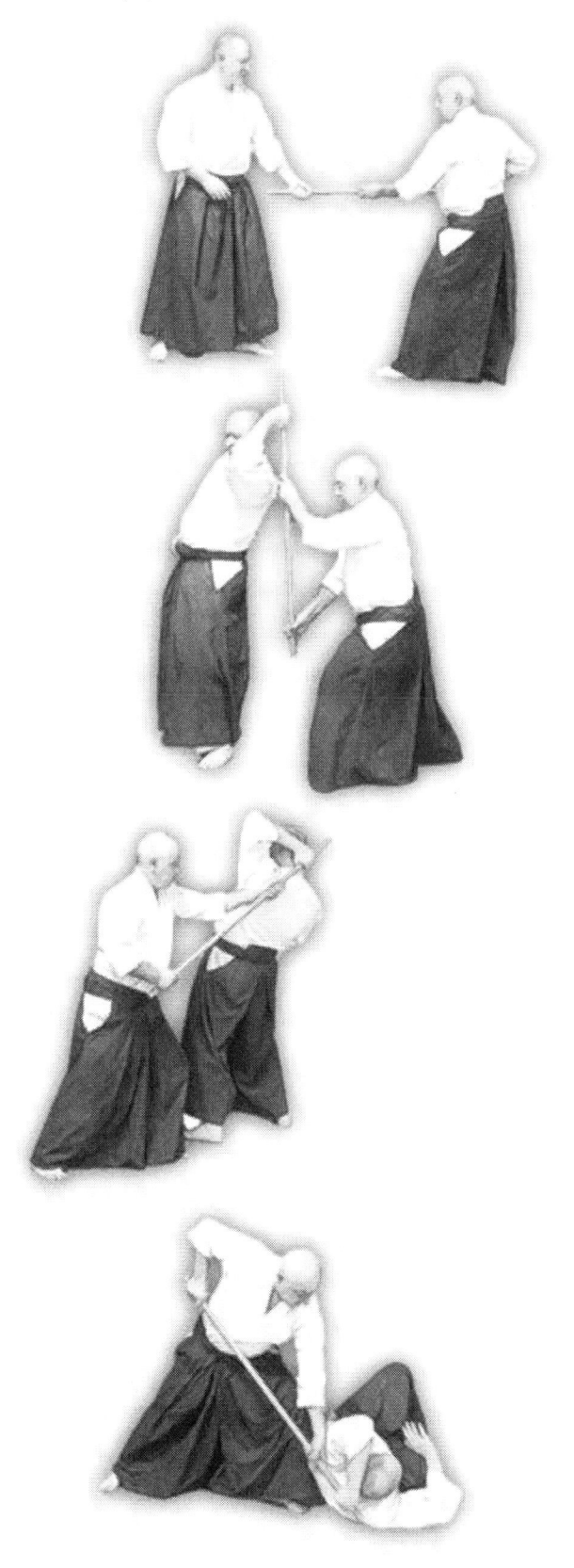

1) *Uke* takes hold of the *jo* with his left hand.

2) You move forward and extend the end of the *jo* upwards.

3) You step forward on your right leg, pass underneath the *jo* and turn 180°.

4) Finally you direct *uke* backwards to the mat.

Part 5: Jo waza

Part 6: Kumijo

Kumijo are paired exercises in which you learn to attack and defend applying the *suburi* shown in Part 2. Initially they should be practised slowly and carefully, only gradually increasing the speed. Many of these *kumijo* are incorporated into the paired sequence at the end of this section to show how they can be combined for attack and defence.

Kumijo #1

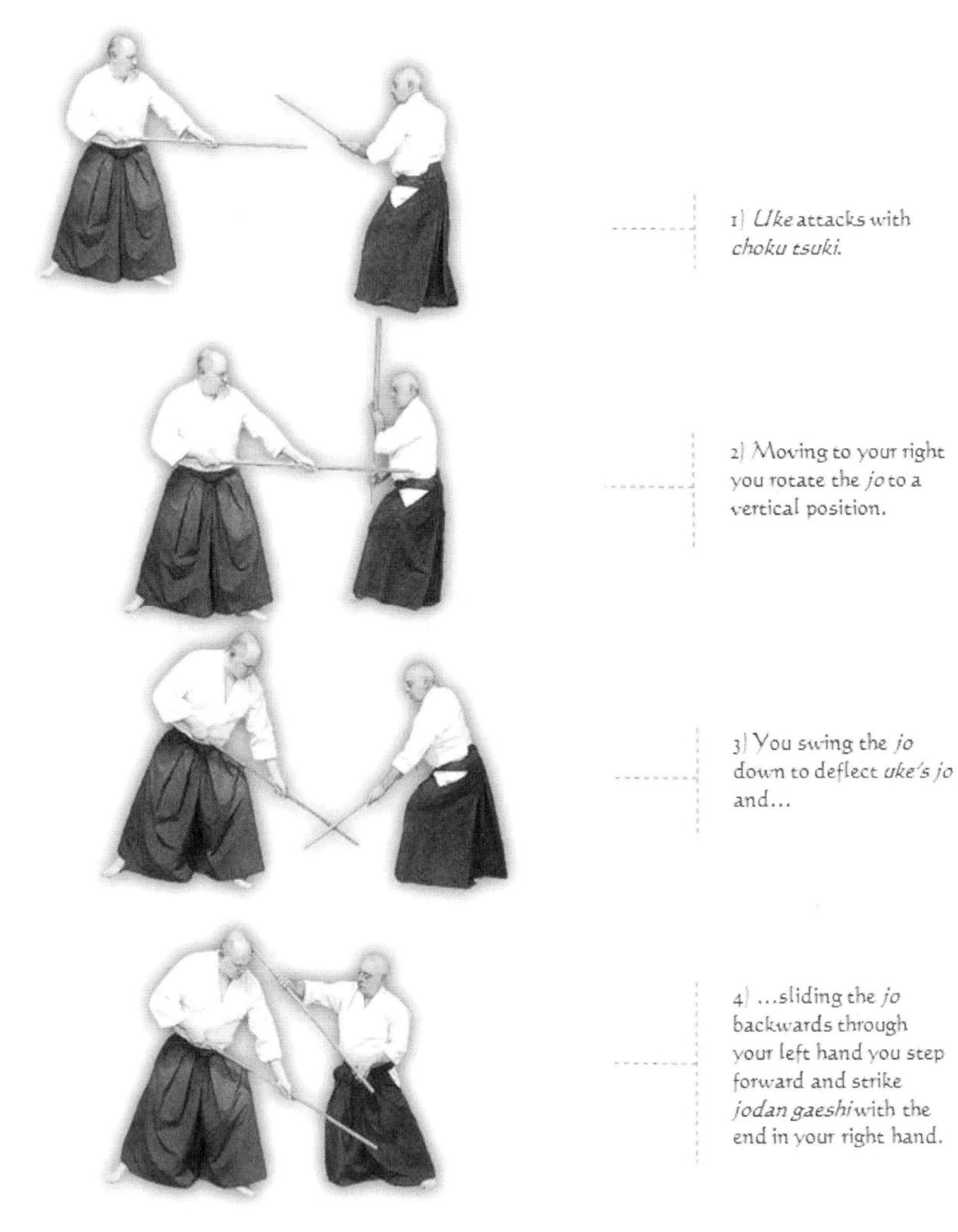

1) *Uke* attacks with *choku tsuki*.

2) Moving to your right you rotate the *jo* to a vertical position.

3) You swing the *jo* down to deflect *uke's jo* and...

4) ...sliding the *jo* backwards through your left hand you step forward and strike *jodan gaeshi* with the end in your right hand.

Kumijo #2

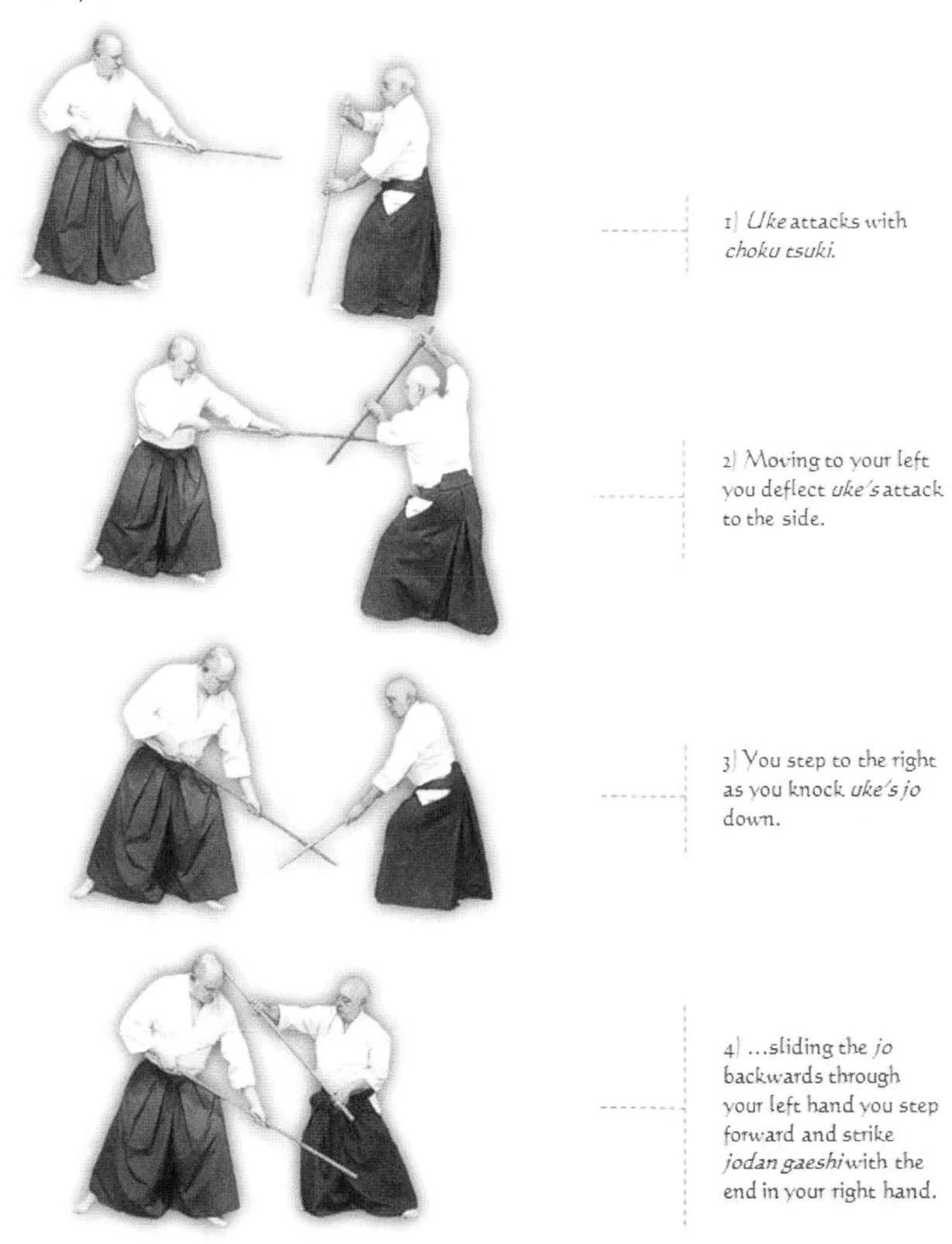

1) *Uke* attacks with *choku tsuki*.

2) Moving to your left you deflect *uke's* attack to the side.

3) You step to the right as you knock *uke's jo* down.

4) ...sliding the *jo* backwards through your left hand you step forward and strike *jodan gaeshi* with the end in your right hand.

Kumijo #3

1) *Uke* attacks with *choku tsuki*.

2) Moving to your right you you deflect *uke's* attack to the side.

3) You step forward and strike *with choku tsuki*.

Part 6: Kumijo

Kumijo #4

1) *Uke* attacks *jodan tsuki*.

2) Moving to your right and to your rear you intercept *uke's* attack.

3) You step to the right as you move your right hand towards your left hand, rotate the *jo* behind you and take hold of the forward end with your left hand.

4) You step forward and strike *shomen uchi*.

Kumijo #5

1) *Uke* attacks with *jodan tsuki*.

2) Moving back, out of range, you deflect *uke's* attack downwards.

3) ...sliding the *jo* backwards through your left hand you step forward and strike *shomen uchi*.

Kumijo #6

1) *Uke* attacks *jodan tsuki*.

2) Moving to your rear you intercept *uke's* attack.

3) You counter with *jodan tsuki* and uke deflects the attack, stepping to his right.

4) *Uke* strikes *yoko gedan*, aiming for your front (left) knee.

5) You block the attack. As you step back on your left leg.

# Kumijo #7

1) *Uke* attacks *jodan tsuki*.

2) Moving to your rear you intercept *uke's* attack.

3) You slide the *jo* through your left hand as you drop the *jo* behind your head.

4) You step diagonally forward on your right leg and attack *toma katate gedan gaeshi*.

Kumijo #8

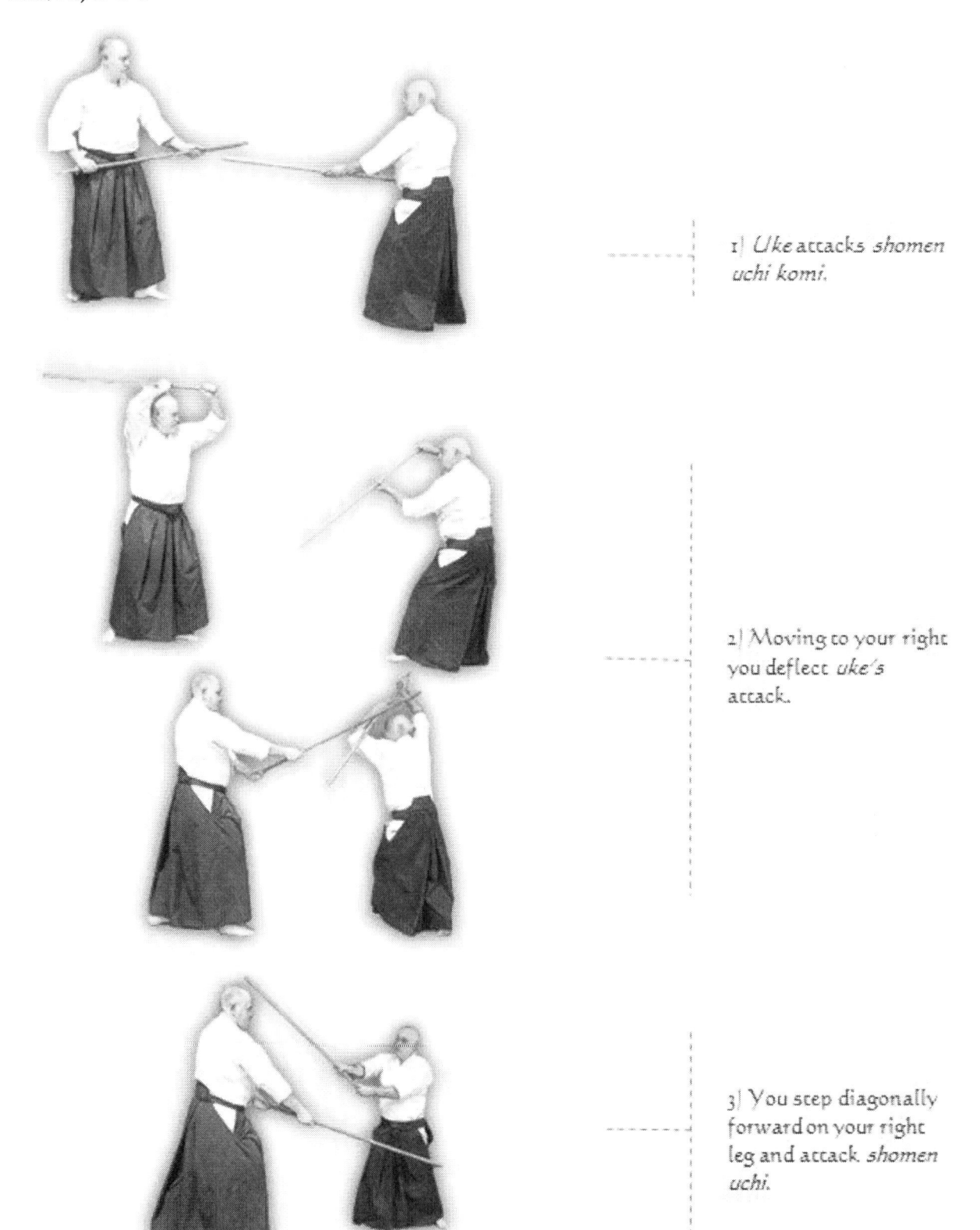

1) *Uke* attacks *shomen uchi komi*.

2) Moving to your right you deflect *uke's* attack.

3) You step diagonally forward on your right leg and attack *shomen uchi*.

Kumijo #9

1) *Uke* attacks *shomen uchi komi*.

2) Moving to your left you deflect *uke's* attack.

3) You counter with *choku tsuki*.

Kumijo #10

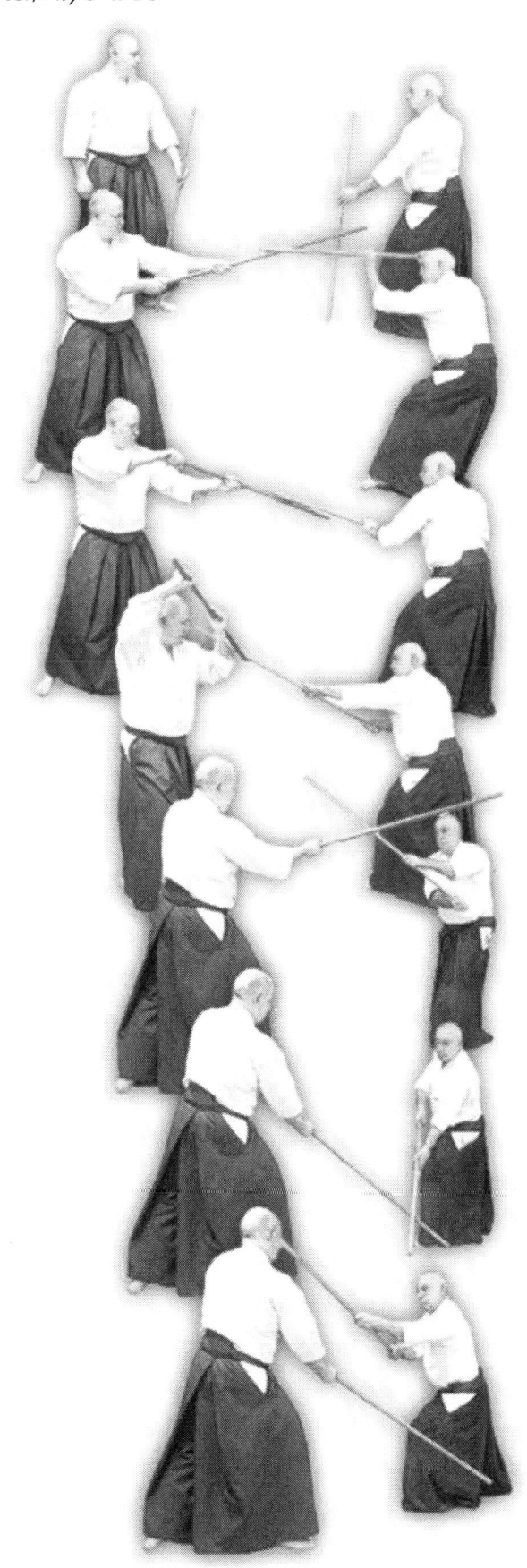

1) *Uke* attacks *jodan tsuki*.

2) Moving to your back you intercept *uke's* attack and counter attack with *jodan tsuki*.

3) *Uke* parries and attacks *yokomen uchi*.

4) You parry and counter with *jodan gaeshi*.

Kumijo #11

1) *Uke* attacks *jodan tsuki*.

2) Moving to your back you intercept *uke's* attack and counter attack with *jodan tsuki*.

4) *Uke* parries and attacks *yokomen uchi*. You parry and deflect his *jo* downwards.

5) You counter with *choku tsuki*.

Part 6: Kumijo

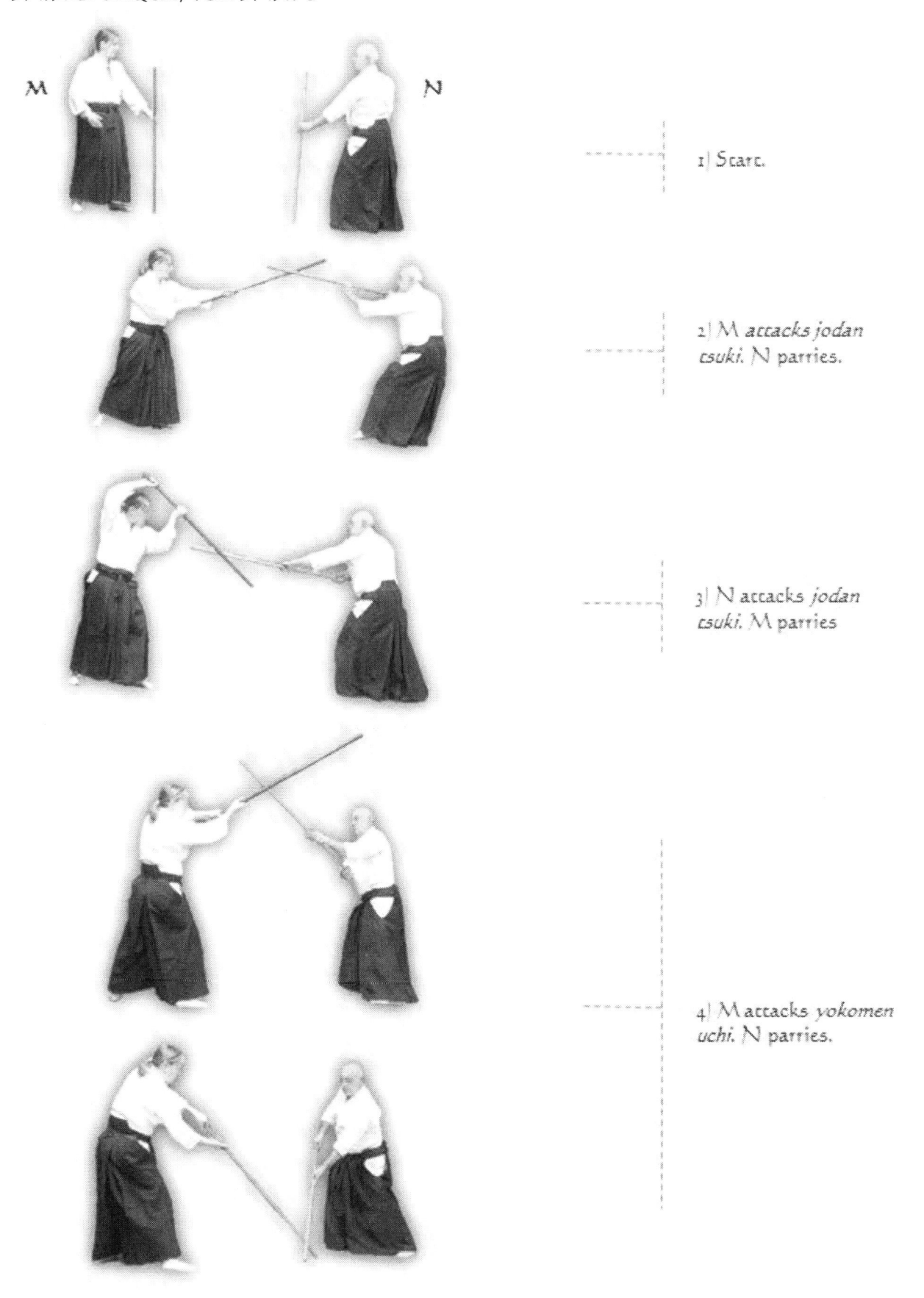

PAIRED SEQUENCE PART 1

1) Start.

2) M attacks *jodan tsuki*. N parries.

3) N attacks *jodan tsuki*. M parries

4) M attacks *yokomen uchi*. N parries.

PAIRED SEQUENCE PART 1

[87]

Part 6: Kumijo

Part 1... cont.

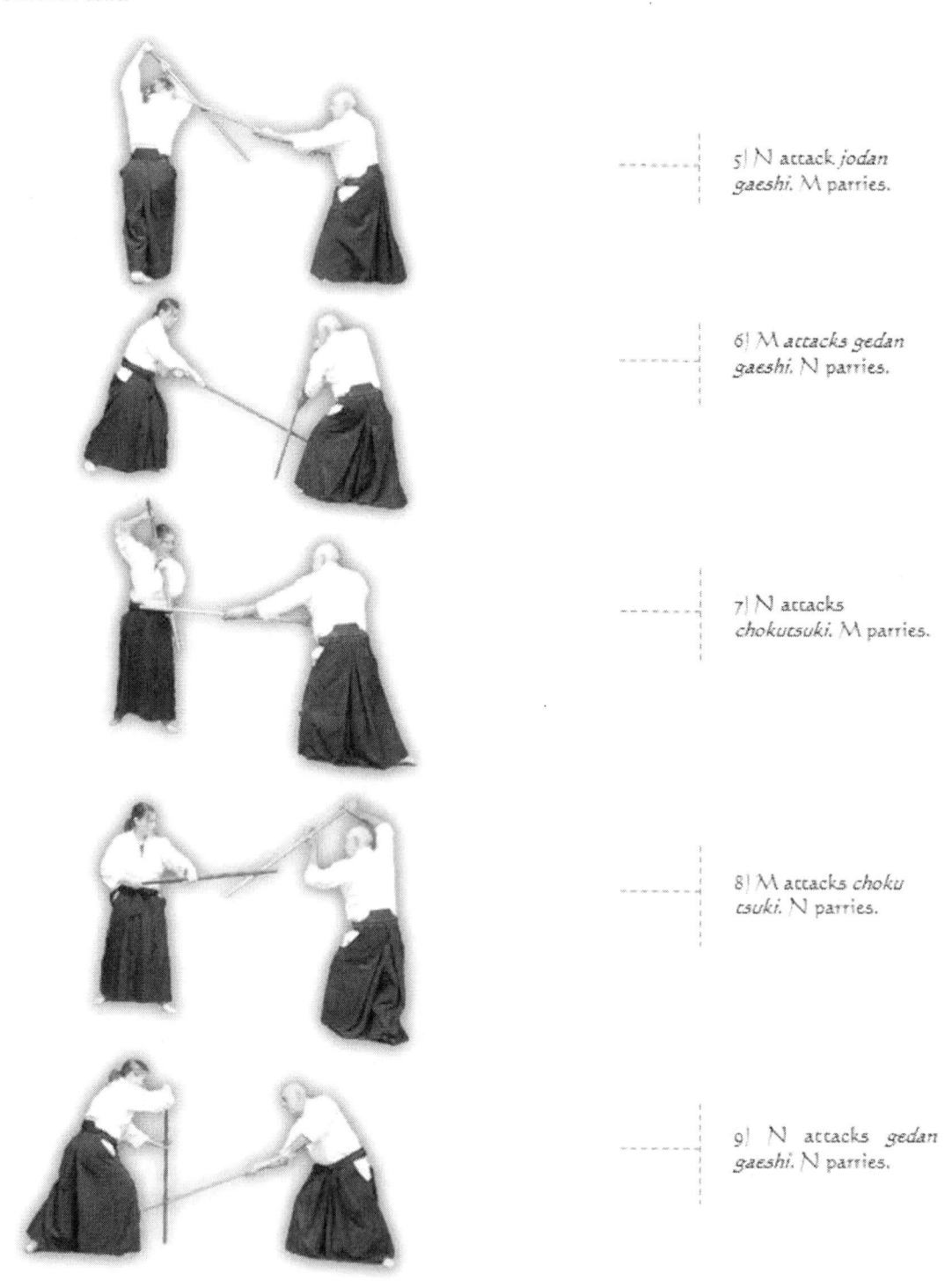

5) N attack *jodan gaeshi*. M parries.

6) M attacks *gedan gaeshi*. N parries.

7) N attacks *chokutsuki*. M parries.

8) M attacks *choku tsuki*. N parries.

9) N attacks *gedan gaeshi*. N parries.

Part 6: Kumijo

Part 1... cont.

10) M attacks *shomen uchi*. N parries and assumes *hasso* stance.

11) M attacks *choku tsuki*. N parries.

Part 1... cont.

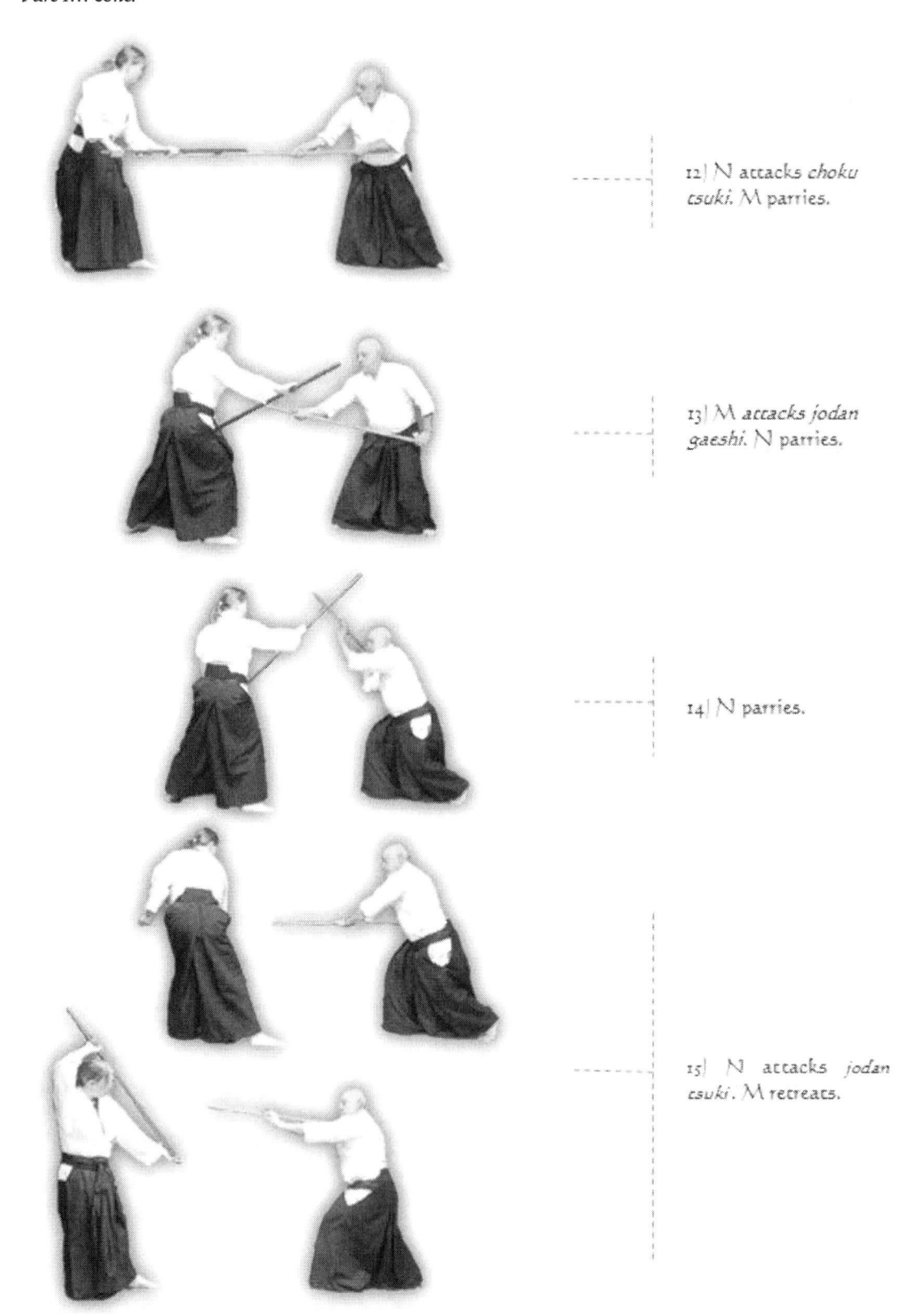

12) N attacks *choku tsuki*. M parries.

13) M attacks *jodan gaeshi*. N parries.

14) N parries.

15) N attacks *jodan tsuki*. M retreats.

Part 6: Kumijo

PAIRED SEQUENCE PART 2

16) M attacks *toma katate gedan gaeshi*. N parries.

17) N attacks *shomen uchi*. M parries.

18) M attacks *choku tsuki*. N parries.

Part 6: Kumijo

Part 2... cont.

19) N attacks *yokomen uchi*. M parries.

20) M attacks *shomen uchi*. N parries.

21) N attacks *yokomen uchi*. M ducks.

22) M attacks *choku tsuki*..

Part 6: Kumijo

Part 2... cont.

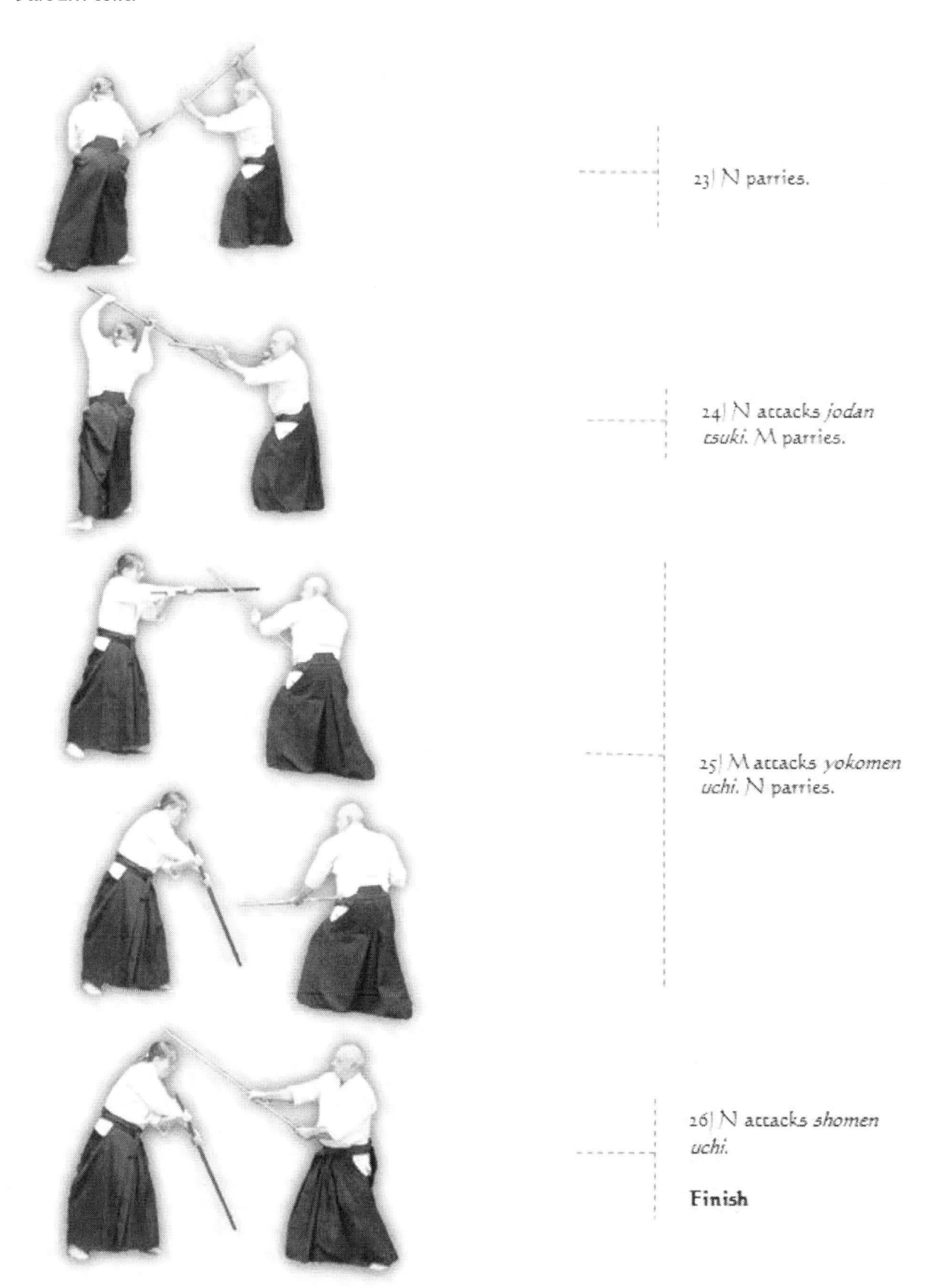

23| N parries.

24| N attacks *jodan tsuki*. M parries.

25| M attacks *yokomen uchi*. N parries.

26| N attacks *shomen uchi*.

Finish

Glossary

Term	Pronunciation	Meaning
Aikido	Aye-kee-dough	Harmony ki way
Choku tsuki	Cho-koo tskee	Straight thrust
Chudan barai	Choo-dan barr-eye	Mid-section parry
Chudan tsuki	Chew-dan tskee	Punch to mid-section
Dojo	Dough-joe	Practice room
Gedan barai	Geddan bar-eye	Lower section parry
Gedan gaeshi	Geddan gay-she	Lower section circular strike
Gyaku yokomen uchi	Gee-akoo yoe-koe-men	Reverse side head strike
Hachi no ji	Hachee no jee	Figure of eight jo swing
Hasso gaeshi	Hasso gay-she	Jo position vertical at shoulder
Ikkyo	Ikkyoe	First form
Irimi tenkan	Irrimmee tenkan	Step forward with full turn
Jo dori	Joe dorree	Uke attacks with jo
Jo kata	Joe katta	Solo sequence of movements
Jo suburi	Joe soo-boo-ree	Single attack or defence with jo
Jo waza	Joe wazza	Uke attempts to take the jo from tori
Jodan barai	Joe-dan bar-eye	High-level parry
Jodan tsuki	Joe-dan tskee	Punch to head
Ju san kata	Jew-san katta	Thirteen count jo kata
Kaeshi tsuki	Kie-shee tskee	Circular thrust
Kaiten	Kie-ten	Turn
Kata gatame	Katta gat-ammay	Arm entanglement
Kokyu	Koe-kyoo	Breath
Kokyu ho	Koe-kyoo hoe	Exercise involving movement while being held
Kokyu nage	Koe-kyoo naggay	A throw using focussed power
Kotegaeshi	Koe-tay-gie-shee	Small hand-turn
Kumijo	Koo-mee joe	Paired exercises with jo
Migi-hanmi	Miggee han-mee	Right posture
Nana no kata	Nanna no katta	Seven count jo kata
Nikyo	Nikyoe	Second form
San ju ichi no kata	San jew itch no katta	Thirty-one count jo kata
Sankyo	Sankyoe	Third form
Shihonage	Shee-hoe naggay	Four-direction throw
Shomen uchi	Show-men oochee	Top head strike
Shomen uchikomi	Show-men oochee kommy	Vertical strike while stepping forward
Tai sabaki	Tie sabbakee	Body movements
Tenkan	Tenkan	Full turn pivoting on front foot
Toma katate gedan gaeshi	Toe-ma kat-attay geddan gay-she	Sweeping circular low strike
Toma katate uchi	Toe-ma kat-attay oochee	Sweeping circular upward strike
Tori	Torry	Defender/performer of technique
Uchi	Oo-chee	Strike
Uke	Oo-kay	Attacker
Ushiro tsuki	Oo-she-roe tskee	Thrust to rear
Yokomen uchi	Yoe-koe-men oochee	Side head strike

Printed in Great Britain
by Amazon